MW00814188

Business Continuity Planning Methodology

Business Continuity Planning Methodology

Dr. Akhtar Syed Ph.D., CISSP, CBRP
Afsar Syed BMath., ABCP, CBRP

National Library of Canada Cataloguing in Publication

Syed, Akhtar, date-
        Business continuity planning methodology / Akhtar Syed, Afsar Syed.

Includes bibliographical references and index.
ISBN 0-9733725-0-8

        1. Crisis management. 2. Emergency management. 3. Business planning.
I. Syed, Afsar, date- II. Title.

HD49.S84 2003   658.4'056   C2003-905952-9

Business Continuity Planning Methodology

ISBN 0-9733725-0-8

Suggestions for improvements to this book are welcome. Please send your comments and suggestions to info@sentryx.com.

www.sentryx.com   1-800-869-8460.

To Narmeen, Imaud, Khurrum, and Wafa.

Contents

Preface

The business continuity planning process (BCP process) consists of six key stages:

1. Risk management
2. Business impact analysis
3. Business continuity strategy development
4. Business continuity plan development
5. Business continuity plan testing
6. Business continuity plan maintenance

Although there are many publications that explain business continuity planning, very few provide detailed methods on how to implement it; even fewer cover implementation of all six stages.

The purpose of writing this book is to provide readers a single, comprehensive, text that explains the principles of BCP and presents an easy to follow step-by-step methodology to implement its six stages. The methodology is consistent with business continuity industry standards, guidelines, and best practices such as ISO/IEC 17799, NFPA 1600, COBIT, and DRI International. Our goal is to give readers the skills to manage risks, conduct a business impact analysis, develop a business continuity strategy, and develop, test, and maintain a business continuity plan.

The methodology considers protection of mission critical business processes, resources, and services. It focuses on various key resources including IT systems and infrastructure, manufacturing and production equipment and products, facilities, work areas, vital records, and critical data.

This book is an excellent resource for those who develop business continuity plans, manage business continuity projects, or want to learn about the subject of BCP. It is a valuable reference for people seeking certifications such as CISSP (Certified Information Systems Security Professional), CBRP (Certified Business Resilience Professional), or CBCP (Certified Business Continuity Professional).

Chapter 1
Introduction

1.1 Chapter Overview

Disasters can strike quickly and without warning. Webster's dictionary defines disaster as:

> "a calamitous event, especially one occurring suddenly and causing great loss of life, damage, or hardship, as a flood, airplane crash, or business failure" [1].

Floods, earthquakes, tornadoes, and hurricanes are examples of major calamitous events.

Businesses are vulnerable to the impact of not only major calamities but also minor business disruptions[1]. Factors such as increased dependency on technology and "speed to market" pressures have made

---

[1] Throughout this book, the terms disruption, business disruption, disruptive event, and disaster are used interchangeably and refer to an event ranging from a minor business interruption to a major calamity.

businesses sensitive to even minor disruptions. Some examples of minor disruptive events are power outages, information technology (IT) system failures, manufacturing equipment failures, hazardous material contamination, voice and data communication failure, and computer viruses.

Over the past decade, the risks of natural disasters, technical and accidental failures, and malicious activities have increased the possibility of business disruptions. In spite of increased risks, studies show that many businesses have remained complacent. According to Gartner, "... many enterprises that experience a disaster never recover. Gartner estimates that two out of five enterprises that experience a disaster go out of business within five years" [2]. These findings reflect the failure of businesses to invest in adequate disaster planning and preparations.

Serious consequences of business disruptions can be avoided through business continuity planning (BCP). BCP is a discipline that prepares an organization to maintain continuity of business during a disaster through an implementation of a business continuity plan. A business continuity plan is a document that contains procedures and guidelines to help recover and restore disrupted processes and resources to normal operational status within an acceptable time frame.

This book explains the concept of BCP with a specific emphasis on the process and methodology for developing, maintaining, and implementing a business continuity plan.

The methodology considers people, business processes, and resources as essential elements of a business continuity plan. A business continuity plan cannot function effectively without the collective efforts of the people assigned to various roles and responsibilities defined in the plan. Continuity of business cannot be maintained without the continuous support of critical business processes—tasks and operations performed by business units or functions—and various resources required by these processes.

Figure 1-1 depicts the typical resources involved in a business conti-nuity plan, namely, IT infrastructure, data centers, manufacturing and production facilities, critical machinery and equipment, critical records, office work areas, critical data, voice and data communication infrastructure, and off-site storage facilities.

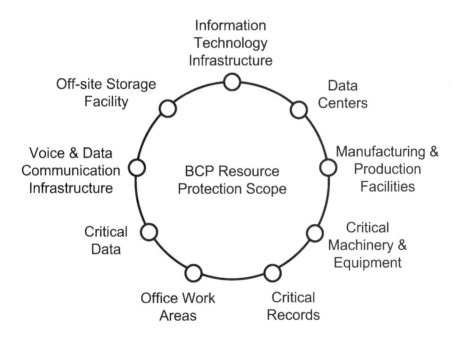

Figure 1-1: Typical resources considered in a business continuity plan

The remainder of this chapter discusses the following aspects:

- Reasons for BCP;
- Relationship of BCP and other planning approaches;
- BCP concepts;
- BCP process, best practices, and guidelines;
- Overview of BCP products and deliverables; and
- Roadmap for the rest of the book.

1.2 Reasons for BCP

Surviving the damaging impacts of unexpected disruptive events is the main reason for businesses to implement BCP. The importance of BCP is clearly demonstrated by the recent World Trade Center (WTC) disaster that directly impacted many businesses within the WTC and its vicinity [3] [4]. Businesses that had untested, outdated, or no business continuity plans suffered enormous financial and operational impacts [5]. Merrill Lynch—a financial management company with headquarters located across from the WTC—is one of the few organizations that continued business as usual. Their success in surviving the WTC disaster was attributed to their up-to-date and extensively tested business continuity plan.

BCP helps businesses survive disruptive events by protecting their key areas of vulnerabilities, such as:

- **Loss of or Injury to Personnel**
  The loss of life suffered from events such as the WTC disaster provides a compelling reason for many businesses to include safety of employees within the scope of their BCP. Traditionally, safety of employees has been addressed as part of crisis

management planning (see Section 1.3 *BCP and Other Planning Approaches* for a discussion of crisis management planning and BCP). At the very least, BCP must be integrated and coordinated with an existing crisis management plan.

- **Implications of Rules and Regulations**
  BCP helps organizations to comply with various laws and regulations and helps to avoid the penalties of non-compliance. Examples of laws and regulations related to business continuity planning are

  1. Foreign Corrupt Practices Act (FCPA),
  2. Gramm-Leach-Bliley Act (GLBA),
  3. Comptroller of Currency Banking Circulars and Federal Financial Information Examination Council (FFIEC),
  4. Computer Security Act of 1987,
  5. Electronic Fund Transfer Act (EFTA), and
  6. Joint Commission on Accreditation of Health Organizations (JCAHO).

  See Appendix 1A *BCP Related Rules and Regulations* for a detailed discussion of these laws and regulations.

- **Loss of Revenue**
  Businesses have concerns of losing significant revenues from both major and minor operational disruptions. A major disaster that disrupts the business for days is very likely to have a devastating impact on revenue. A minor disruption that lasts for several hours can cause considerable loss of revenue for businesses with real-time sales and service transactions.

- **Damage to Critical Resources**
  To support a company's mission, business functions and opera-

tions rely on various critical resources such as IT systems, manufacturing and production equipment, critical records, and voice and data communication infrastructure. Protecting such resources from the damaging effects of disaster is one of the key objectives of BCP.

- **Loss of Customers**

  In today's business environment, customers demand highly efficient service and timely delivery of products. Losing dissatisfied customers to competitors as a result of a business disruption is a major concern of organizations. One of BCP's objectives is to recover disrupted critical processes and services in time to avoid loss of customers to competitors.

- **Civil and Criminal Liabilities**

  An organization and its management can be held accountable to their customers, business partners, and shareholders for failing to take proper actions to prevent or mitigate the effects of a disaster. BCP helps to reduce the civil or criminal liabilities for an organization and its management.

- **Damage to Reputation**

  The effects of a disaster can extend beyond the loss of assets and revenue to damage to a company's image and reputation. BCP helps businesses recover from a disaster within a time frame that reduces damage to its reputation.

1.3 BCP and Other Planning Approaches

Organizations have traditionally relied on different types of planning approaches to protect their businesses and assets from the impacts of a disaster. The following are some of the common types of planning approaches [14] [15] [16] [17]:

- **Disaster Recovery Planning (DRP)**
  DRP focuses on the recovery of IT services and resources in the event they are disrupted by a major disaster.

- **Business Resumption Planning (BRP)**
  BRP deals with resumption of business processes effected by an IT application outage, through the use of work-around procedures.

- **Continuity of Operations Planning (COOP)**
  COOP aims to recover the strategic functions of an organization that are performed at its headquarters facility. These functions, which exclude IT applications and services, are performed at an alternate recovery site for a maximum period of up to thirty days.

- **Contingency Planning (CP)**
  CP focuses on the recovery of IT services and resources following a major disaster or a minor system disruption. It specifies procedures and guidelines for recovery at both on-site and off-site (alternate) facilities.

- **Emergency Response Planning**
  The objective of emergency response planning is to safeguard employees, public, environment, and the organization's assets,

and to bring the crisis situation under control immediately following a crisis event.

Limited focus is a common weakness of these planning approaches. Each planning approach focuses on the protection of specific aspects of an organization, while ignoring other critical areas. To address this limitation, an integrated planning approach is needed to protect all of the critical areas of an organization. BCP has emerged as a framework that integrates the scope and objectives of all of these approaches [16] [18] [19].

Crisis events of the recent past have contributed to the expansion of the scope and objectives of BCP, which have been historically associated with the scope and objectives of DRP. The experience gained from these crises suggests that the scope of BCP needs to include not only IT services and resources, but also social behavior, business processes, accidental failures, and major catastrophic events.

One example that shows how traditional planning failed to account for the effects of disaster on personnel is the recent ice storm of 1998 that affected Canada and parts of the United States. In this situation, the companies' staff members stayed away from work due to concerns about their families. An important lesson learned from these events is that the human component must not be ignored in disaster planning.

An example that shows the lack of business process support in most of the IT-centric recovery plans is the WTC (World Trade Center) attack of September 11, 2001. The plans used during this disaster overlooked the importance of manual functions performed by various functional units such as sales, finance, and payroll. In addition to their reliance on computer infrastructure, these manual functions relied on paper records, forms, and documents.

1.4 Business Continuity Planning Concept

Conceptually, BCP can be divided into two areas:

1. Business continuity planning management (BCP management)

2. Business continuity planning process (BCP process)

Figure 1-2 depicts the activities of BCP management and BCP process on a time line relative to a business disruption.

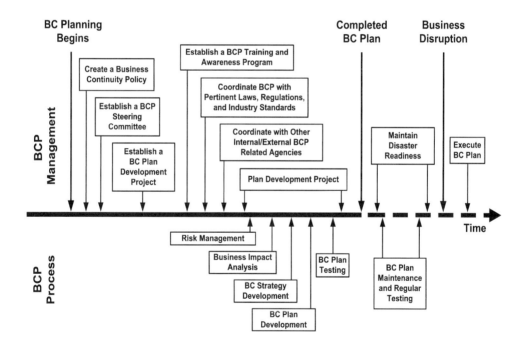

**Figure 1-2: A time line of BCP activities
relative to a business disruption**

BCP management focuses on management and organizational components of BCP. Some of the key activities of BCP management are:

- Issue an organization-wide business continuity policy that
  directs management and staff of each business unit to take
  responsibility for maintaining continuity of critical business
  functions and processes in the event of a business disruption.

- Establish a steering committee with members from senior management to define the BCP scope, provide ongoing BCP support
  and direction, monitor BCP status and progress, and allocate
  BCP funding.

- Initiate a formal project for developing a business continuity
  plan that covers the entire organization.

- Ensure that personnel involved in the development and implementation of the business continuity plan are adequately
  trained. Develop and implement a BCP awareness and training
  program for the entire organization.

- Ensure that BCP is in compliance with pertinent government
  laws and regulations, and industry standards.

- Coordinate BCP activities with relevant disaster recovery and
  business continuity agencies and local authorities.

- Ensure that the business continuity plan remains in a state of
  readiness at all times.

- Execute the business continuity plan at the time of disaster.

Together, BCP management and BCP process enable an organization to develop a business continuity plan, maintain it in a constant ready-state, and execute in the event of a business disruption.

The BCP process defines a life cycle for developing and maintaining a business continuity plan. The BCP process life cycle model consists of the following stages:

1. **Stage 1—Risk Management**
   Stage 1, risk management, assesses the threats of disaster, existing vulnerabilities, potential disaster impacts, and identifies and implements controls needed to prevent or reduce the risks of disaster.

2. **Stage 2—Business Impact Analysis (BIA)**
   Stage 2, business impact analysis, identifies mission-critical processes, and analyzes impacts to business if these processes are interrupted as a result of a disaster.

3. **Stage 3—Business Continuity Strategy Development**
   Stage 3, business continuity strategy development, assesses the requirements and identifies the options for recovery of critical processes and resources in the event they are disrupted by a disaster.

4. **Stage 4—Business Continuity Plan Development**
   Stage 4, business continuity plan development, develops a plan for maintaining business continuity based on the results of previous stages, specifically, risk management, BIA, and business continuity strategy development.

5. **Stage 5—Business Continuity Plan Testing**
   Stage 5, business continuity plan testing, tests the business
   continuity plan document to ensure its currency, viability, and
   completeness.

6. **Stage 6—Business Continuity Plan Maintenance**
   Stage 6, business continuity plan maintenance, maintains the
   business continuity plan in a constant ready-state for execution.

Stages 1 through 5 are part of the "Plan Development Project" activities of BCP management. Stage 6 is part of "Maintain Disaster Readiness" activity of BCP management.

1.5 BCP Process: Best Practices and Industry Guidelines

The BCP process, described in the preceding section, is consistent with business continuity best practices and industry guidelines. Figure 1-3 shows the life cycle model of the BCP process.

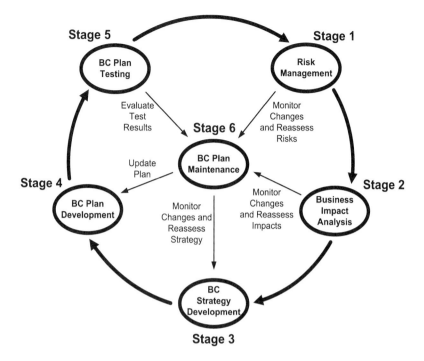

Figure 1-3: Six stages of the BCP process

The BCP process life cycle begins with risk management followed in sequence by business impact analysis, business continuity strategy development, business continuity plan development, and business continuity plan testing. The results of each stage are used as input for the next stage. Business continuity plan maintenance is an ongoing activity which monitors people, resources, and technological changes and updates the business continuity plan as needed.

The BCP process is closely associated with business continuity best practices and guidelines such as:

- **DRI International (DRII)**
  DRI International (DRII) defines six stages in its BCP model [19]. Risk analysis and control, business impact analysis and

time-sensitive business functions, and alternative business continuity strategies are all part of the functional requirements phase. These correspond to the first three stages in Figure 1-3, namely, risk management, business impact analysis, and business continuity strategy development.

The third and fourth phases of the DRII model—the Design and Development phase and the Implementation phase—correspond to the business continuity plan development stage in Figure 1-3; the fifth phase—the Testing and Exercising phase—corresponds to the testing stage in Figure 1-3; and the sixth phase of the DRII model—the Maintenance and Updating phase—corresponds to the maintenance stage in Figure 1-3.

- **National Fire Protection Association (NFPA)**
  NFPA 1600 is a standard on Disaster/Emergency Management and Business Continuity Programs which is issued by the National Fire Protection Association (NFPA) [17]. NFPA 1600 is endorsed by the Federal Emergency Management Agency (FEMA). The six stages of BCP process life cycle can be mapped to the specific subject matters described in the NFPA 1600 standard. The activities of the risk management stage of the BCP process life cycle are contained within the hazard identification and risk assessment, hazard mitigation, and resource management elements of the NFPA 1600 standard. The activities of the business continuity strategy development stage and the BIA stage are similar to the "Mitigation Plan" and the "Business Impact Analysis" elements of NFPA 1600 standard, respectively. The business continuity plan development stage is related to the "Recover/Business Continuity Plan" part of the standard and the testing and maintenance stages are addressed in the "Exercises, Evaluations & Corrective Actions" element of the standard.

- **International Organization for Standardization (ISO)**
  ISO/IEC 17799 is an international standard for Information Security Management issued by the International Organization for Standardization (ISO) [22]. Business continuity management, one of its ten security controls, emphasizes the need for a managed process to develop and maintain business continuity throughout the organization. The elements of this managed process include the six stages of BCP process life cycle. The first element deals with understanding risks, which is similar to the risk management stage. The second element, Business Continuity and Impact Analysis, corresponds to the business impact analysis stage. The third element which deals with the formulation and documentation of a business continuity strategy is similar to the business continuity strategy development stage of the BCP process. The fourth element addresses the formulation and documentation of a business continuity plan and maps to the business continuity plan development stage of the BCP process. The fifth element, which includes regular testing and updating of plans and processes, corresponds to the testing and maintenance stages of the BCP process.

1.6 Key Deliverables of the BCP Process

At the conclusion of each stage of the BCP process, a report or a
document is delivered which summarizes the analysis and activities of
that stage. The information contained in a deliverable from one stage
becomes a basis for the analysis and activities involved in the next
stage of the BCP process, as Figure 1-4 illustrates.

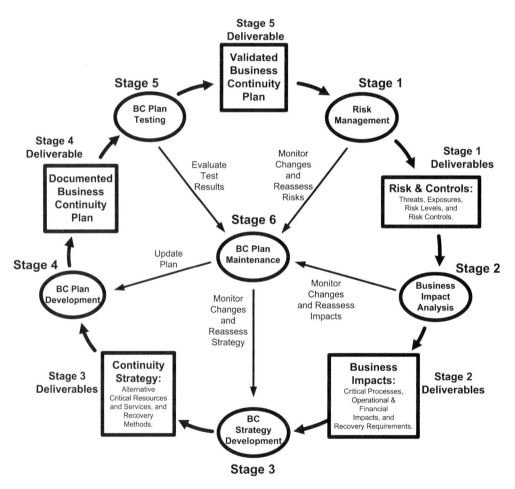

Figure 1-4: Key deliverables of the BCP process

The following list summarizes the key deliverables of the BCP process:

- **Risk Assessment Report**

  A risk assessment report, which is an outcome of stage 1 of the BCP process, identifies business disruption threats, exposures, and risks. This report also contains recommendations to control the risks of business disruption.

- **Business Impact Analysis (BIA) Report**

  Stage 2 delivers a BIA report that identifies areas of the business that are mission-critical, the extent of the potential operational and financial impact of a business disruption, and requirements for recovering from a business disruption.

- **Business Continuity Strategy Report**

  As an outcome of Stage 3 of the BCP process, the business continuity strategy report identifies viable options for recovering resources and services in the event they are impacted by a business disruption.

- **Business Continuity Plan Document**

  A business continuity plan is the product of Stage 4 of the BCP process. It contains procedures and guidelines needed to recover and restore damaged resources and disrupted business processes. Stage 5 tests the accuracy and validity of the plan. Stage 6 ensures that the plan is maintained in a constant ready-state for execution, through updates of the plan on a continuous basis.

1.7 Roadmap to this Book

The remainder of this book is organized according to the six stages of the BCP process: risk management, business impact analysis, business continuity strategy development, business continuity plan development, business continuity plan testing, and business continuity plan maintenance.

Chapter 2 *Risk Management,* presents a risk management framework for assessing risks to continuity of business operations and for developing and implementing controls to avoid or reduce risks to acceptable levels. The chapter is organized in two main parts. The first part introduces the key concepts of risk and explains methods for risk assessment. The second part describes the risk management framework in detail.

Chapter 3 *Business Impact Analysis*, introduces business impact analysis (BIA) concepts; clarifies the relationship between risk assessment and BIA; lists the benefits of a BIA; describes the methods for conducting a BIA; and explains various pieces of information needed for a BIA in the context of a disaster-to-recovery time frame. The rest of this chapter is devoted to a step-by-step process for conducting a BIA. The BIA process consists of several steps which analyze the impact of disruption to the normal business operations and identify the requirements to restore mission-critical processes.

Chapter 4 *Business Continuity Strategy Development*, describes a framework for developing a business continuity strategy. The framework begins with identification of recovery requirements and ends with a set of recovery options for the business continuity strategy. This chapter also identifies general considerations for developing a recovery strategy and provides strategy related recommendations for recovery contracts and service level agreements.

Chapter 5 *Business Continuity Plan Development*, provides guidance for developing a business continuity plan. The chapter describes the type of information a plan must include to be effective for maintaining business continuity if a disaster occurs. The chapter introduces phases involved in the implementation of the business continuity plan—initial response and notification, problem assessment and escalation, disaster declaration, plan implementation logistics, recovery and resumption, and restoration. This chapter includes a discussion on the requirements for an emergency response plan.

Chapter 6 *Business Continuity Plan Testing*, explains the key concepts of business continuity plan testing and provides a structured framework for developing an effective business continuity test plan. The purpose of the business continuity test plan is to aid the preparation and execution of business continuity plan tests.

Chapter 7 *Business Continuity Plan Maintenance*, addresses the business continuity plan maintenance stage. It describes various activities needed to ensure that the business continuity plan always remains accurate, current, complete, and in a ready-state for implementation.

Chapter 8 *BCP Process: Reports and Documents Summary* concludes the discussion of the preceding chapters by presenting a summary of the information and knowledge gained through the BCP process.

Appendix A *BCP Standards, Guidelines, and Best Practices* provides a summary of key published documents that contribute to a common body of knowledge for BCP.

Appendix B *Business Continuity Resource Information*, provides information on and links to business continuity planning organizations, natural hazard and disaster organizations, and business continuity publications.

Lastly, this book has a glossary containing a list of commonly used
BCP terms, a reference section containing a list of references used in
this book, and an index at the end of this book.

Appendix 1A: BCP Related Rules and Regulations

The Foreign Corrupt Practices Act (FCPA) of 1977 [6] contains provisions that prohibit publicly held companies in the United States from bribing foreign officials. In conjunction with the anti-bribery provisions, FCPA also contains accounting provisions that mandate companies to maintain and safeguard accurate business transaction records. Violations of the FCPA provisions can result in criminal penalties for corporations, business entities, officers, directors, stockholders, employees, and agents. The criminal penalties range from fines of up to $2,000,000 and prison terms for up to five years.

The Gramm-Leach-Bliley Act (GLBA) [7], known as the Financial Services Modernization Act of 1999, includes directives for financial institutions to ensure security and confidentiality of customers' financial and personal information, and to protect such confidential information against potential threats and hazards.

Financial institutions must comply with Comptroller of Currency Banking Circulars and Federal Financial Information Examination Council (FFIEC) guidelines such as BC 177 (1983; revised July 1987) [8], BC 187 [9], FIL-68-97 [10]. The banking circulars and FFIEC guidelines require financial institutions to implement corporate-wide contingency planning which addresses not only information technology but also key operational areas. FFIEC guidelines, in particular, specify the financial institutions' boards of directors and senior management as those responsible for ensuring corporate-wide implementation of contingency planning.

The Computer Security Act of 1987 [11] mandates federal agencies to establish a security plan to protect sensitive information from the risk of loss, misuse, and unauthorized access and modification.

The Electronic Fund Transfer Act (EFTA) [12] defines the basic rights, liabilities, and responsibilities of consumers and organizations that participate in electronic fund transfer systems. According to this Act, a participating organization is liable to a consumer for all damages resulting from the organization's failure to make an electronic fund transfer in the correct amount or in a timely manner.

The Joint Commission on Accreditation of Health Organizations (JCAHO) requires accredited health organizations to adapt its Emergency Management Standards [13]. These standards call on JCAHO accredited organization to address the risk of all potential hazards and threats through development and implementation of an emergency management plan. The accredited health organizations are also expected to test their emergency management capabilities through at least one community-wide annual drill.

Chapter 2
Risk Management

2.1 Chapter Overview

Fires, floods, earthquakes, IT system failures, and equipment breakdowns are a few examples of events that threaten businesses with potentially disastrous consequences—such as loss of lives, damaged facilities, inoperable systems and equipment, financial losses, and environmental damages. By ignoring various threats and their adverse consequences, organizations expose themselves to unwarranted risk of business interruptions. While it is often difficult to completely eliminate such risks, organizations can reduce them to acceptable levels through effective use of risk management methods.

The chapter is organized into two main parts. Section 2.2 *Risk Concepts* introduces the key concepts of risk and explains methods for risk assessment. Section 2.3 *Risk Management Framework* describes a risk management framework and its seven phases. Appendix 2A *Risk Assessment*

Data Collection Process at the end of this chapter explains the process of collecting the data needed in the first phase of the risk management framework (*Risk Assessment*).

2.2 Risk Concepts

Risk concepts help to explain, measure, and assess risks and they must be able to address these requirements:

- Capture what is meant by the term *risk* through a representation of risk and its components
- Define metrics for measuring risk
- Define methods for risk assessment

These requirements are addressed in Section 2.2.1 through to Section 2.2.3:

- Section 2.2.1 *Risk Representation* describes risk through its components and their relationships.
- Section 2.2.2 *Risk Measurement Metrics* explains two commonly used metrics for measuring risk.
- Section 2.2.3 *Risk Assessment Methods* describes two common methods for assessing risks corresponding to the metrics explained in Section 2.2.2.

2.2.1 Risk Representation

Risk is a part of our everyday activities, for example, an accident caused by a driver under the influence of alcohol. In this example, risk can be characterized in terms of these components:

- **Threat**—possibility of an accident caused by a drunk driver; and
- **Consequences**—the accident results in damage to the car, loss of life, or personal injury.

Threat and its consequences are the two main components central to the definition of risk. Figure 2-1 represents the risk of a car accident through its two components.

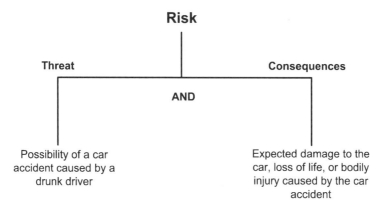

Figure 2-1: Representation of risk for the car accident example

Depending on the risk assessment and management requirements, the threat component of risk can be further decomposed into subcomponents to convey additional threat related information such as

- the likelihood of the threat,
- the threat event,
- the source of the threat, and
- the category of the threat source.

Figure 2-2 expands the threat component in Figure 2-1 to show the threat subcomponents. The car accident represents the threat event, and the drunk driver represents the threat source. The likelihood of the threat is expressed as the probability that a drunk driver will cause a car accident. Figure 2-2 assumes this probability to be 60 percent, that is, the drunk driver will cause an accident 6 out of 10 times that he/she drives the car.

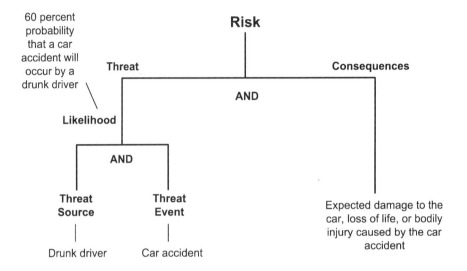

Figure 2-2: Decomposition of the threat component into its subcomponents

Threat sources are classified into three general categories: natural, technical, and human. For instance, the threat source (drunk driver) for the car accident example belongs to the human threat source category. Table 2-1 in Step 1 *Threat Source Identification* of Section 2.3.1 *Risk Assessment* lists examples of natural, technical, and human threat sources.

The representation of risk used to describe the car accident example is applicable to business related risk as well. Consider an ice storm scenario which threatens the power supply of a business. The business depends on the power supply to support its office facility and computer center.

Figure 2-3 captures the risk associated with the ice storm scenario. In this figure, the ice storm represents the threat source. The threat event is the power outage resulting from the ice storm. As a consequence of the power outage, the computer center and the office facility could become partly inoperable. The loss is expected to be $2.5 million in lost revenue. This example assumes that the likelihood of the power outage to be once every four years or 25 percent in an annualized term.

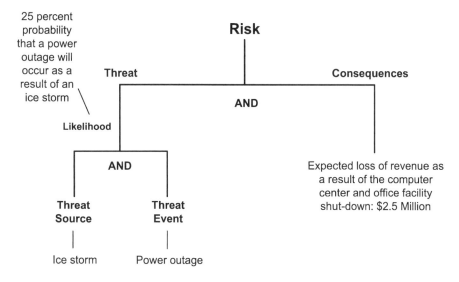

Figure 2-3: Representation of an example business risk

2.2.2 Risk Measurement Metrics

There are two basic categories of risk metrics used for measuring and comparing risks: quantitative and qualitative. Quantitative metrics use numerical values to measure risks, such as a value of $250,000 used for the annualized risk of damage to a building due to a threat of an earthquake. Compared to the quantitative metrics, the qualitative metrics use values such as low, medium, or high to describe the annualized risk of damage to the building structure due to a threat of an earthquake.

Figure 2-4 uses quantitative metrics to represent the risk described in the ice storm example. The consequence of the power outage is stated in quantitative terms as an expected loss of $2.5 million. Based on this loss and probability value of 25 percent, the risk value is expressed quantitatively as $625,000.

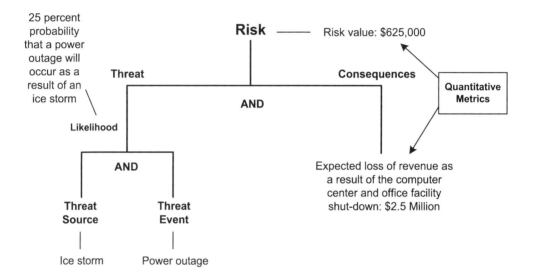

Figure 2-4: An example of risk using quantitative metrics

Figure 2-5 shows the risk involved in the ice storm example using qualitative metrics. The consequence of the power outage is stated in a qualitative term as a "high" business impact. The risk is also expressed qualitatively as a value of "low" which is derived from the "high" business impact and the threat probability of 25 percent.

Qualitative risk metrics involve simpler computations and require less time compared to the quantitative metrics. Their main drawback is that the risk values are subjective and non-repeatable because they are based on judgments.

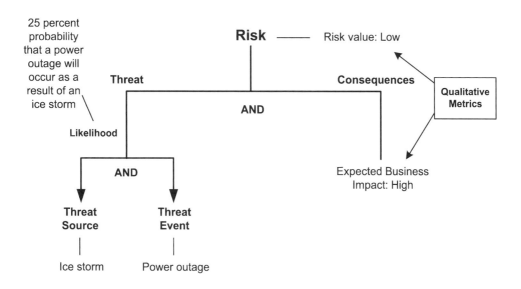

Figure 2-5: An example of risk using qualitative metrics

Quantitative risk metrics are derived algorithmically using probability and other mathematical functions. Their main limitation is that considerable time and effort are required to gather and analyze data, and to explain the results.

2.2.3 Risk Assessment Methods

A risk assessment method determines the risk value based on the values for the likelihood and the consequences of a threat. Annualized Loss Expectancy (ALE) and Annualized Impact Expectancy (AIE) are two examples of risk assessment methods. These methods differ with respect to the types of metrics used to determine the risk values. The ALE method is based on quantitative metrics, whereas, the AIE method uses qualitative metrics.

AIE is suited for situations where the consequences of threats can be characterized quantitatively. For cases in which the quantitative data is complex and difficult to obtain, AIE is a more viable option compared to ALE.

Annualized Loss Expectancy (ALE) Method

ALE determines risk values based on the values of its two components:

1. Annualized Rate of Threat Occurrence (ART)
2. Single Loss Expectancy (SLE)

Figure 2-6 shows a mapping of the ALE method's components to the components of risk described in Section 2.2.1 *Risk Representation*.

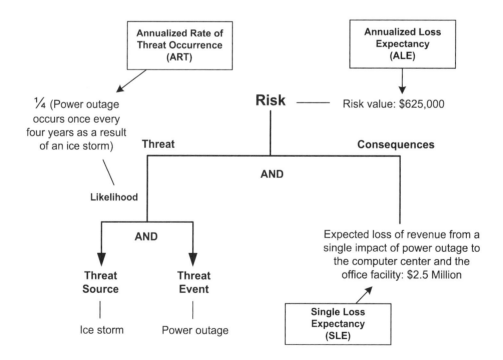

Figure 2-6: A mapping of ALE components to the risk representation

According to the mapping, ART refers to the threat likelihood as an annualized term, and SLE represents the consequence for a single impact of the threat. In addition, the Annualized Loss Expectancy value corresponds to the risk value.

The value of ALE is derived from ART and SLE using the formula

>   ALE = Single Loss Expectancy (SLE) * Annualized Rate of Threat Occurrence (ART)

where

>   Single Loss Expectancy (SLE) = Asset Loss Potential Value (ALPV) * Exposure Factor (EF).

The Asset Loss Potential Value (ALPV) measures the potential for a monetary loss if the entire asset is impacted by a threat event. The Exposure Factor (EF) indicates the percentage of the Asset Loss Potential Value exposed to a single occurrence of a threat event.

For the ice storm example, assume that the loss potential is $10 million, if the entire computer system within the computer center is impacted by the power outage. In other words, the ALPV is $10 million. The exposure factor is assumed to be 25 percent of the ALPV for a single occurrence of power outage. According to the formula above, the SLE is calculated as

$10,000,000.00 * 25/100 = $2,500,000.

The ice storm may occur at a rate of once every four years. The Annualized Rate of Threat Occurrence (ART) is therefore ¼. Given these values of SLE and ART, ALE is computed as

$2,500,000 * ¼ = $625,000.

Annualized Impact Expectancy (AIE) Method

The AIE method measures risk in qualitative terms based on the values of its two components:

1. Annualized Rate of Threat Occurrence (ART)
2. Single Impact Expectancy (SIE)

Figure 2-7 shows a mapping of the AIE method's components to the components of risk as described in Section 2.2.1 *Risk Representation*. According to this mapping, ART refers to the likelihood of the threat as an annualized term, and SIE represents the consequence for a single impact of

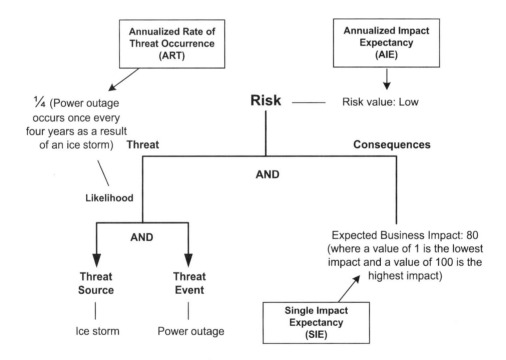

Figure 2-7: Relationship between AIE method and risk value, threat likelihood, and consequences

the threat as a qualitative numeric value. In addition, the Annualized Impact Expectancy value corresponds to the risk value.

The value of AIE is derived from ART and SIE using the formula

> AIE = Single Impact Exposure (SIE) x Annualized Rate of Threat Occurrence (ART)

where SIE expresses the impact of a single threat event occurrence as a numeric value. For instance, SIE can be represented with a value selected from 1 to 100 such that a rating of 1 represents lowest impact and a rating of 100 indicates highest impact. The meaning of ART is the same as it is used in the ALE calculation.

For the ice storm example, assume that the expected rate of an ice storm is once every four years. The annualized rate of threat occurrence (ART) is therefore ¼. The magnitude of the impact is considered to be high with a numeric SIE value of 80 because of the critical operational importance of the computer center to the entire organization. Based on the values of SIE and ART, the AIE is

$80 * ¼ = 20.$

The numeric AIE value can be mapped to a more meaningful qualitative term by creating a mapping between the range of values and qualitative terms. A simple example of this mapping is given below:

- High: if the numeric value is between 67 and 100
- Medium: if the numeric value is between 34 and 66
- Low: if the numeric value is between 1 and 33

According to the above mapping, the power outage caused by an ice storm is considered a "low" risk to the organization.

2.3 Risk Management Framework

This section describes a risk management framework for assessing risks to business continuity and for developing controls either to prevent risks from occurring, or to reduce their impact to acceptable levels. The framework is divided into seven phases as depicted in Figure 2-8. The phases in the framework are

- Phase I: Risk Assessment,
- Phase II: Risk Control Options Assessment,
- Phase III: Risk Controls' Cost and Effectiveness Assessment,
- Phase IV: Risk Reporting,
- Phase V: Risk Control Decision,
- Phase VI: Risk Control Implementation, and
- Phase VII: Risk Monitoring and Control.

The outputs from phases I, II, and III are used in Phase IV to prepare a report of the risk assessment to management. Theses outputs include the following information:

1. **Threats to Business Continuity**
   Phase I identifies potential threats to the organization.

2. **Risks Associated with the Threats**
   Phase I determines the consequences, exposed critical assets, and magnitude of risk corresponding to each threat.

3. **Options Available for Controlling Risks**
   Phase II assesses the options available for eliminating or reducing the risks identified in Phase I.

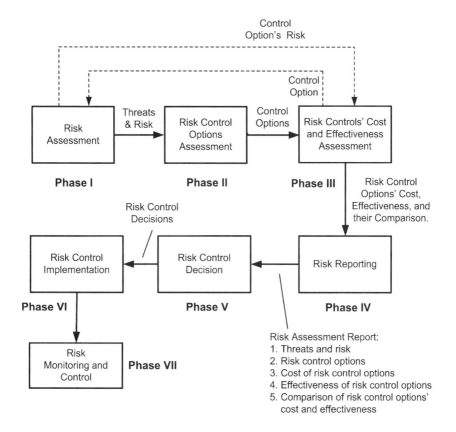

Figure 2-8: Risk management phases

4. Cost of Risk Control Options

Phase III estimates the cost of implementing the control options identified in Phase II.

5. Effectiveness of Risk Control Options

Phase III measures the effectiveness of risk control options by assessing, through the use of Phase I, the expected reduction in the magnitude of risk if the control options are implemented.

6.**Comparison of Costs and Effectiveness of Control Options**
    Phase III compares the cost of implementing risk control options
    with the effectiveness of risk control in reducing the risk.

In Phase V, management reviews the report and decides which options are
appropriate for controlling the threats. The decision is based on the assessment and comparison of the implementation costs and the effectiveness
of the options in reducing the risk. Phase VI implements the risk control
options selected in the preceding phase. Phase VII is an on-going process
that monitors and controls risks to the organization.

2.3.1 Phase I: Risk Assessment

Risk assessment is a process that begins with the identification of potential
threats to an organization and ends with a set of risk values for those
threats. Figure 2-9 describes a risk assessment process consisting of six
main steps:

    Step 1: Identify Threat Sources
    Step 2: Identify Threat Events
    Step 3: Identify Consequences
    Step 4: Assess Single Loss (or Impact) Expectancies
    Step 5: Assess Likelihoods
    Step 6: Derive Risk Values

The risk assessment process is founded on the risk concepts introduced in
Section 2.2 *Risk Concepts*, and it accommodates both the ALE and AIE
methods as explained in Sections 2.2.3 *Risk Assessment Methods*. Before starting this phase, either ALE or AIE methods must be selected.
Appendix 2A of this chapter describes a process of collecting the data
needed to conduct the assessment in this phase.

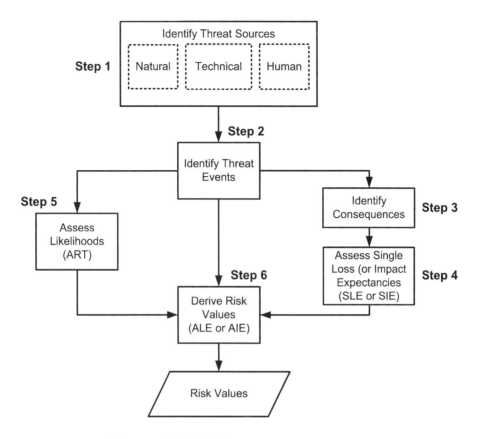

Figure 2-9: Risk assessment process

Step 1: Identify Threat Sources

The first step in the risk assessment process is to identify a list of potential sources of threat to an organization. The output of this step is a list of threat sources from natural, technical, and human threat source categories. Table 2-1 shows examples of threat sources and their categories.

Natural Threats	Technical Threats	Human Threats
Fire	Electrical power disruption	Hacker
Earthquake	Computer disk failure	Computer virus
Tornado	Computer server failure	Disgruntled employee
Snow storm	Software application bug	Robbery
Ice storm	Heating and air-conditioning equipment failure	Vandalism
High wind	Voice or data communication service failure	Terrorism
Volcanic eruption	Water or gas plumbing leaks	Work related accident (Chemical spill, Fire, etc.)
Deadly disease epidemic	Energy shortage	Work place violence
Typhoon	Network failure	Arson
Flood	Plane crash	Strike
Heat wave	Nuclear disaster	War

Table 2-1: Threat source categories and example threat sources

Step 2: Identify Threat Events

Step 2 determines the threat events that can occur as a result of the threats identified in Step 1. The output of Step 2 is a list of threats represented as a combination of threat source and threat event. Table 2-2 lists three examples of threat events as an example output of Step 2. A power outage and unsafe driving conditions are two possible events that can occur as a result of an ice storm. The power outage occurs when the power lines are damaged by the ice. The unsafe driving condition occurs when roads become icy from the ice storm. Another example of a threat source is a hacker who obtains unauthorized access to the company's e-commerce website.

Threat Source	Threat Event
Ice storm	Power outage
Ice storm	Unsafe driving conditions
Hacker	Unauthorized e-commerce website access

Table 2-2: Example output of Step 2

Step 3: Identify Consequences

Step 3 determines the consequences of threats identified in steps 1 and 2. In addition to the threats, a list of assets that are critical to the organization are required in Step 3 to assess the damage. The assets generally include business processes, information, and resources (such as systems, equipment, and people).

For each threat event, Step 3 first selects the assets (from the list of assets) that can be impacted by the threat event. Next, Step 3 describes the consequences in terms of the ways these assets can be affected by the threat event.

The following is an example list of assets assumed to be critical to the organization:

1. Computer center
2. Staff
3. Clients' personal information

Table 2-3 summarizes the consequences identified in Step 3 for the list of threats in Table 2-2, and the critical assets exposed to these threats.

Threat Source	Threat Event	Critical Asset	Consequence
Ice storm	Power outage	Computer center	Computer systems shutdown
Ice storm	Unsafe driving conditions	Staff	Shortage of staff
Hacker	Unauthorized access to the company's e-commerce site	Clients' personal information	Unauthorized access to personal information

Table 2-3: Examples of threat consequences

A power outage can impact the computer center (a critical resource) leading to a shutdown of its computer systems. The ice storm can also impact the staff (a critical resource) if the road conditions become unsafe and prevent staff from travelling to work. Therefore, a consequence of unsafe road conditions is a shortage of staff. An unauthorized access to the company's e-commerce website by a hacker may result in an unauthorized exposure of clients' personal information.

The output of Step 3 is a list of exposed critical assets and consequences corresponding to the list of threats identified in Step 2.

Step 4: Assess Single Loss (or Impact) Expectancies

Step 4 measures the consequence of a threat (identified in Step 3) as either a Single Loss Expectancy (SLE) or a Single Impact Expectancy (SIE), depending on the choice of ALE or AIE risk assessment method determined at the beginning of Phase I. Both SLE and SIE are described in Section 2.2.3 *Risk Assessment Methods*. Section 2.2.3 also explains the ALE and AIE risk assessment methods.

The SLE quantitatively measures the portion of the overall value of the critical asset and resources exposed to the risk. Figure 2-6 shows the SLE as $2.5 million for the ice storm example (see *Annualized Loss Expectancy (ALE) Method* in Section 2.2.3 *Risk Assessment Methods*). It assumes that the computer center's Asset Loss Potential Value is estimated to be $10 million with a 25 percent Exposure Factor.

The SIE measures the exposure of the critical assets to the consequences (or impact) of a threat event in qualitative terms such as low, medium, and high. Figure 2-5 describes the exposure of computer center to the impact of a power outage with an SIE value of "high" (see *Annualized Impact Expectancy (AIE) Method* in Section 2.2.3 *Risk Assessment Methods*).

The output of Step 4 is a list of

- threat consequences, and their
- Single Loss Expectancy (SLE) values or Single Impact Expectancy (SIE) values.

Step 5: Assess Likelihoods

Step 5 assesses the likelihood of a threat as the Annualized Rate of Threat Occurrence (ART). As explained in Section 2.2.3 *Risk Assessment Methods*, ART represents the likelihood of a threat occurrence in an annualized term. In Figure 2-6, ART is represented with a value of ¼ to indicate that a power outage (caused by an ice storm) can occur once every four years.

The output of Step 5 is a list of ART values corresponding to the threats identified in Step 2.

Step 6: Derive Risk Values

Based on the output of steps 2, 4, and 5, Step 6 computes the risk value using either the ALE or the AIE method. Both ALE and AIE methods are explained in Section 2.2.3 *Risk Assessment Methods*. The ALE is derived using the formula

> ALE = Single Loss Exposure (SLE) * Annualized Rate of Threat Occurrence (ART)

where SLE and ART are outputs of Step 4 and Step 5, respectively.

The AIE is derived as

> AIE = Single Impact Expectancy (SIE) * Annualized Rate of Threat Occurrence (ART)

where SIE and ART are outputs of Step 4 and Step 5, respectively.

The output of Step 6 is a list consisting of

- threats,
- threat consequences, and
- risk values.

Table 2-4 shows the result of Step 6 for the ice storm example using the ALE method. Table 2-5 shows the result of Step 6 for the ice storm example using the AIE method and the following mapping of qualitative terms to numeric values:

- High: if the numeric value is between 67 and 100
- Medium: if the numeric value is between 34 and 66
- Low: if the numeric value is between 1 and 33

Result of Step 6				ALE Components	
Threat Source	Threat Event	Consequence	Risk Value: ALE	SLE	ART
Ice storm	Power outage	Computer system shutdown	$625,000 ($2.5M x ¼)	$2.5M	¼

Table 2-4: Result of Step 6 with the ALE method

Result of Step 6				AIE Components	
Threat Source	Threat Event	Consequence	Risk Value: AIE	SIE	ART
Ice storm	Power outage	Computer system shutdown	Low (or a numeric value of 20 = 80 x ¼)	High (or a numeric value of 80)	¼

Table 2-5: Result of Step 6 with the AIE method

2.3.2 Phase II: Risk Control Options Assessment

Phase II of the risk management framework identifies available options for controlling the risks of threats assessed in Phase I. Risk control options can be divided into four different categories:

1. **Risk Acceptance**—accept the risk and do nothing

2. **Risk Avoidance**—avoid the risk altogether

3. **Risk Reduction**—reduce the risk to an acceptable level

4. **Risk Transfer**—transfer the risk to another entity or organization (e.g. to an insurance company or service provider)

A **risk acceptance** control option may be adopted as a control if, for instance, all other options are extremely costly. Another reason for accepting risk is when a threat has a negligible risk associated with it.

The most preferred control option is **risk avoidance**, but in many cases it may be either impractical or cost prohibitive.

A **risk reduction** control option is the preferred option next to a risk avoidance control option. The first step in reducing risk is to determine an acceptable risk level for a given threat; the second step is to explore control options that lower the current risk level to the acceptable level.

A **risk transfer** control option is used to transfer the risk to another organization that can compensate for the loss or impact caused by a disruptive event. For instance, risk can be transferred to an insurance company through an insurance policy that covers the losses from a disruptive event. Risk can also be transferred to a service provider through an agreement that requires the service provider to compensate the organization for any service disruption.

Risk transfer can be used in conjunction with risk reduction—risk is reduced to a certain level through risk reduction, and the remaining risk is addressed through risk transfer.

As an example application of this phase, consider an organization that delivers mail and parcels overnight and has its facility directly next to an airport—where the risk of a plane crash is considerably higher than locations that are away from the airport. Table 2-6 lists four risk control options for this example.

The first option belongs to the risk avoidance control category. This

	Risk Control Options	Risk Control Category
1	Relocate the main facility to a safe distance away from the airport	Risk Avoidance
2	Relocate the main facility to a location a few miles away from the airport	Risk Reduction
3	Distribute the main facility over three different locations spread around the airport	Risk Reduction
4	Purchase a plane crash insurance policy	Risk Transfer

Table 2-6: Examples of risk control options

option avoids the risk by relocating the main facility to a safe area away from the airport.

The second and third options are from the risk reduction control categories. The second option reduces the risk of a plane crash by relocating the main facility to an area only a few miles away from the airport. Similarly, the third option reduces the risk by distributing the main facility to three different locations spread around the airport.

The fourth option is from the risk transfer control category. This option transfers the risk by purchasing an insurance policy that covers the losses to the organization resulting from a plane crash.

The cost and effectiveness of the options in Table 2-6 are explored in the next section.

2.3.3 Phase III: Risk Controls' Cost and Effectiveness Assessment

The control options identified in Phase II can differ in their implementation cost and in their effectiveness in controlling the risk. The objective of Phase III is to assess the cost and effectiveness of the control options identified in Phase II.

There are three main steps in Phase III. The first step estimates the total cost of implementing the risk control option; the second step assesses the effectiveness of control options in reducing the current risk; and the third step compares the cost with the effectiveness of control options.

Step 1: Cost of Control Options

The total cost for an option is measured in monetary value and includes the costs related to

- equipment/material,
- shipping,
- service and labor,
- taxes,
- insurance,
- rent, and
- maintenance.

Table 2-7 lists the example costs for implementing the options of Table 2-6.

The cost of options 1 and 2 is estimated to be $200 M, which are the highest costs compared to the costs of other options, because both involve relocation of the entire main facility to another location. The cost of imple-

	Risk Control Options	Risk Control Category	Option Cost
1	Relocate the main facility to a safe distance from the airport	Risk Avoidance	$200 M
2	Relocate the main facility to a few miles away from the airport	Risk Reduction	$200 M
3	Distribute the main facility over three different locations spread around the airport	Risk Reduction	$50 M
4	Purchase a plane crash insurance policy	Risk Transfer	$100 M over 20 year period (or $5 M per year)

Table 2-7: Examples costs of risk control options

menting option 3 is $50 M and it is much lower than option 1 and 2 because only a part of the main facility is to be relocated. The cost of option 4 is $100 M over a period of 20 years (or $5 M per year) to purchase an insurance policy to cover the losses in the event of a plane crash.

Step 2: Effectiveness of Control Options

To assess the effectiveness of the control options of Table 2-7, the current risk value without any control options must determined first. Table 2-8 shows the results of Step 6 *Derive Risk Values*, of Phase I, for the mail and parcels organization without implementing the risk control options described in Table 2-6.

The risk value (Annualized Loss Expectancy) is estimated to be $20 M with the single loss expectancy (SLE) of $600 M and the likelihood of a plane crash of once in 30 years. The SLE takes into account potential loss of assets and impact from of loss of life such as loss of revenue and legal liabilities.

Threat Source	Threat Event	Consequence	Risk Value: ALE	Likelihood (ART)
Aircrafts	Plane crash	Damage to the main facility and loss of life	$20 M (or $600 M x 1/30)	1/30 (once in 30 years)

Table 2-8: Assessment of risk value for the example threat of a plane crash

Table 2-9 lists new risk values and their effectiveness in reducing the original risk when the risk control options described in Table 2-6 are implemented.

The risk value without implementing any risk control options is $20 M. The new risk values are obtained by applying Phase I, risk assessment, to each control option:

- Option 1 reduces the likelihood of a plane crash from once every 30 years to once every 5000 years. As a result, the risk is reduced to a negligible value of $0.12 M from the current risk of $20 M. The risk reduction is $19.88 M.

- Option 2 achieves a risk reduction of $10 M because the likelihood of a plane crash is reduced to once every 60 years.

	Risk Control Options	Risk Control Category	Option Cost	Option's Risk Value: ALE	Risk Reduction
1	Relocate the main facility to a safe distance from the airport	Risk Avoidance	$200 M	$0.12 M (or $600 M x 1/5000) with a likelihood of once every 5000 years	$19.88 M (or $20 M – $0.12 M)
2	Relocate the main facility to a location a few miles away from the airport	Risk Reduction	$200 M	$10 M (or $600 M x 1/60) with a likelihood of once every 60 years	$10 M (or $20 M - $10 M)
3	Distribute the main facility to three different locations spread around the airport	Risk Reduction	$50 M	$6.7 M (or $600 M x 1/3 x 1/30)	$13.3 M (or $20 M – $6.7 M)
4	Purchase a plane crash insurance policy	Risk Transfer	$100 M over 20 year period (or $5 M per year)	0	$20 M (or $20 M – 0)

Table 2-9: Risk values for examples risk control options

- Option 3 achieves a risk reduction of $13.3 M by distributing the main facility to three different locations, thereby reducing the likelihood of a plane crash by 1/3rd of the current likelihood value of once every 30 years.

- Option 4 achieves a risk reduction of $20 M by compensating for any losses through an insurance policy.

Step 3: Cost-Effectiveness Comparison of Risk Control Options

The purpose of this step is to facilitate the selection of the best risk control options through a comparison of their costs and risk reduction effectiveness values. This section presents an approach that simplifies the comparison of risk control options. The approach focuses on the cost of achieving a unit of risk reduction for each option. The cost per unit of risk reduction is determined by the formula

Cost per Unit of Risk Reduction (CURR)
= Cost of Control Option / Risk Reduction.

The CURR value can help management to select the best option from the risk avoidance, risk reduction, and risk transfer control option categories. A risk control option with a low CURR value is preferred over a risk control option that has a high CURR value. A low CURR value indicates that the cost of reducing the risk is low when compared with a high CURR value. Table 2-10 indicates the Cost per Unit of Risk Reduction for the control options of Table 2-9.

	Risk Control Options	Risk Control Category	Option Cost	Risk Reduction	Cost per Unit of Risk Reduction (CURR)
1	Relocate the main facility to a safe distance from the airport	Risk Avoidance	$200 M	$19.88 M	$10.06
2	Relocate the main facility to a location a few miles away from the airport	Risk Reduction	$200 M	$10 M	$20.00
3	Distribute the main facility to three different locations spread around the airport	Risk Reduction	$50 M	$13.3 M	$3.75
4	Purchase a plane crash insurance policy	Risk Transfer	$100 M over 20 year period (or $5 M per year)	$20 M	$5 (assuming the cost of $100 M over 20 year period)

Table 2-10: Cost per unit of risk reduction for example options

The CURR value for option 3 is the lowest at $3.75. Option 4 has the next lowest CURR value of $5. Option 1 has the third lowest CURR value of $10.06. Option 2 has the highest CURR value of $20.

According to the CURR values, option 3 can be recommended to management as the best risk control option. Because of a relatively small difference between the CURR values of Option 3 and Option 4, Option 4 can also be recommended as the next best option.

In summary, Phase III provides the following information regarding each risk control option:

1. Cost of implementing the risk control option
2. Effectiveness of the risk control option in reducing the current risk
3. CURR value of the risk control option

2.3.4 Phase IV: Risk Reporting

Once phases I, II, and III are completed, Phase IV documents their results in a risk assessment report. The risk assessment report is presented to management and includes the following:

1. Threats and risks identified in Phase I;

2. Critical assets exposed to the threats;

3. For each threat event, a list of risk control options and their categories; and

4. For each risk control option
   a   cost of implementing each risk control option
   b   risk reduction effectiveness
   c   cost per unit of risk reduction (CURR values)
   d   the best risk control options based on their CURR values.

Moreover, the risk assessment report must document

1. the scope of the risk assessment — for example, the scope may define the areas of the business, types of threats, types of critical assets covered by the risk assessment;

2.assumptions used in the risk assessment;

3. the risk assessment method used in the assessment; and

4. the source of data used in the assessment.

Before presenting the risk assessment report to management, the contents of the report must be reviewed to determine the following:

1. Relevance and significance of the threats and risk, identified in the report, to the organization;

2. Validity of the assumptions used in the report;

3. Accuracy of the cost estimated for implementing control options; and

4. Best control options recommended in the report.

The risk assessment report may need revisions and updates in the event that the review reveals errors, inconsistencies, or inaccuracies in risk assessment.

2.3.5 Phase V: Risk Control Decision Process

The risk assessment report prepared in the preceding phase is presented to management in this phase. Management reviews the report and chooses the best risk control option.

The first step in the decision process is to establish a range of Acceptable Risk (AR) values to help with the decision process. The range of AR values indicates the level of risk management is willing to tolerate for any given threat.

The second step in the decision process is to select threats with a tolerable level of risk by comparing their current risk values with the range of the AR values. The risk acceptance control option is adopted for the selected threats if their current risk values are within the range of AR values. In other words, management is willing to accept the risk associated with the selected threat and ignore any options specified in the report for avoiding or minimizing the risk.

The third step in the decision process focuses on threats with current risk values outside the range of AR values. For each of these threats, risk control options that can either reduce the risk to an acceptable level or eliminate it completely are selected as implementation candidates.

The fourth step in the decision process is to determine the single most appropriate risk control option for each threat. This decision can be based on management's objectives such as to ensure that the risk control option for a threat

1. minimizes the cost per unit of risk reduction (or has a low CURR risk value),

2. minimizes disruption to the organization as a result of implementing the risk control option,

3. minimizes the impact to the shareholders,

4. avoids additional operational costs once the control is implemented, and

5. minimizes the length of time and effort needed to complete the implementation.

The outcome of this phase is a range of AR values and a list of risk control options—representing the risk control decisions of management—for each threat identified in the risk assessment report.

2.3.6 Phase VI: Risk Control Implementation

This phase aims to implement the risk control decisions of management. This phase must be tailored to the project implementation guidelines and procedures established by the organization. In general, this phase can be divided into three main steps for each risk control option.

The first step is to conduct a feasibility study for implementing the risk control option. The feasibility study should determine whether or not the control option is operationally, technically, economically viable. The findings of the project feasibility study are documented in a project feasibility report to be presented to the management.

In the second step, the feasibility report and a request for project funding is presented to management. Management reviews the report to decide whether or not to approve the project funding request.

The third step implements the risk control project only if management approves the risk control project and its funding requirements. A complete project implementation plan is developed and executed in this step.

2.3.7 Phase VII: Risk Monitoring and Control

This phase represents an on-going monitoring and control of the changes in the existing threats and addition of new threats to the organization. The risk monitoring and control phase conducts periodic risk assessments and risk audits to evaluate changes in the threats and risks to the organization, and implements appropriate risk control options. Periodic risk assess-

ments and identification of risk control options is achieved through the
methods explained in phases I through VI. Phases IV, V, and VI are used
to select and implement appropriate risk control options. This phase
becomes a part of the BC plan maintenance stage of the BCP process.

Appendix 2A: Risk Assessment Data Collection Process

Phase I risk assessment of the risk management framework involves a process of collecting risk assessment data. This data is used to determine the values for the components of risk:

- Threat source
- Threat event
- Threat likelihood
- Threat consequence

The data collection process for the risk assessment must be based on a thorough analysis of the organization's external and internal areas of risk exposures and concerns. Examples of external areas of risk exposures and concerns for an organization include the following:

1. **Geography**

   Is the company site located in a region with a potential for natural disasters such as earthquakes, tornadoes, and floods?

2. **Proximity**

   Is the company site situated close to a hazardous site such as a nuclear power plant, chemical factory, or an airport?

3. **Accessibility**

   Is the work site difficult to access in the event of a disruption such as a transportation mishap, strike, civil disorder, or bomb threat?

4. **Dependency**

   Is the company dependent on external business partners such as suppliers, customers, and financial institutions?

The following are examples of internal areas of risk exposures and concerns:

1. **Personnel**
    a. Is there a potential for threats from disgruntled employees?
    b. Is there a dependence on rare skilled workers?
    c. Does the work involve risks to an employee's health and safety?

2. **Systems and Equipment**
    a. What is the failure rate of systems and components?
    b. What is the age of the systems and components?
    c. Is there a potential for equipment theft?
    d. Is there a possibility of accidental damage?

3. **Facility**
    a. Are there physical weaknesses in the building plan and structure?
    b. Is there a building security exposure?
    c. Are there electrical hazards within the facility?
    d. Are the plumbing and water supply lines exposed to potentially harmful conditions such as rust or extreme weather?
    e. Is there regular maintenance of heating, ventilation, and air-conditioning systems?

4. **Hazardous Material**
    a. Is there a potential for mishandling of hazardous material?
    b. Is there a potential for hazardous material leaks or spillage?
    c. Are hazardous materials stored in a safe and secure location?

5. **Confidential Data and Vital Records**
    a. What are the threats to confidential data/information and vital records?

    b. Are confidential data and vital records stored in a safe and secure location?

There are a number of sources that can provide the data needed for risk assessment. A list of potential data sources is given below:

- Existing no-smoking and clear-desk policies;
- Existing contingency plans;
- Current safety permits that cover fire alarms, fire extinguishers, fire escape plans, and sprinkler systems;
- UPS and secondary power generators;
- Security monitoring systems;
- Security policies;
- Off-site backup contracts;
- Service level agreements;
- Disaster insurance policies;
- Problem and service maintenance records of systems, equipment, and building infrastructure;
- Known threats identified by private and government sectors;
- Statistics published by disaster control agencies;
- Log of IT security breaches detected through Intrusion Detection System (IDS); and
- History of criminal activities in the region recorded by the local police department.

Chapter 3
Business Impact Analysis

3.1 Chapter Overview

The Business Impact Analysis (BIA), which is conducted in the second stage of the BCP process, analyzes the financial and operational impact of disruptive events on the business areas and processes of an organization. The financial impact refers to monetary losses such as lost sales, lost funding, and contractual penalties. Operational impact represents non-monetary losses related to business operations, and can include loss of competitive edge, damage to investor confidence, poor customer service, low staff morale, and damage to business reputation.

The BIA identifies the following information:

- Mission-critical areas of the business and their processes

- Extent of potential operational and financial impact to the organization
- Requirements for recovering disrupted critical business processes

The findings of the BIA enable an organization to determine the extent of the overall effort needed to recover from a potential business disruption, thereby paving the way for developing the business continuity strategy and business continuity plan.

The main objective of this chapter is to familiarize the reader with the key concepts and elements of the BIA and describe a step-by-step process for conducting it. This chapter is divided into eight sections: Sections 3.2 to 3.7 introduce the key concepts of the BIA; Section 3.8 explains the steps involved in the BIA process; and Section 3.9 concludes the chapter with a discussion of a report to summarize the BIA findings.

3.2 Risk Management and BIA

The risk management stage precedes the business impact analysis stage in the BCP process depicted in Figure 1-3. The risk management stage assesses possible business continuity threats and risks to the organization. The overall objective of the risk management stage is to control these risks through one or more risk control options: risk acceptance, risk avoidance, risk reduction, and risk transfer.

There are many factors associated with the risk control options—such as cost, effort, and feasibility—that often restrict management to only two options: risk reduction or risk acceptance. Both of these options, unfortunately, leave the organization exposed to the "residual risks" of business disruption—risks that remain after implementing risk control options. Hence, the organization needs to develop a business continuity plan that prepares it to deal with the "residual risks".

The BIA is a crucial link between the risk management stage and the business continuity plan development stage. The BIA identifies the mission-critical areas of business and continuity requirements which become the main focus of the business continuity plan.

3.3 BIA Benefits

Business disruptions can have many undesirable consequences such as financial loss, dissatisfied customers, damage to business reputation, and legal liabilities. The findings of the BIA raise management's awareness of these undesirable consequences and therefore the need for a business continuity plan. Hence the BIA is a means for obtaining management's approval for implementing the rest of the BCP process.

The findings of the BIA also identify the requirements for recovering disrupted mission-critical areas and processes of the organization. These recovery requirements become the basis for developing a suitable business continuity strategy and an effective business continuity plan. Moreover, the BIA can help to determine whether or not the existing business continuity strategy addresses the recovery requirements.

The BIA process involves subject matter experts from different parts of the organization, each able to contribute knowledge and expertise of his/her own business area.

By participating in BIA workshop and group meetings, staff can enhance their knowledge of the business and appreciate the importance of business continuity planning.

3.4 Who should be involved in a BIA?

Business continuity is a concern of the entire organization, not just the IT department. Therefore, all areas of the organization should be involved in a comprehensive BIA. At least one representative from each business area of the organization should participate.

The role of the business representative is to understand the BIA process, scope, and objectives thoroughly. The representative participates in BIA interviews and workshops in order to provide the required data and information regarding their own areas. They are responsible for communicating BIA-related information between the BIA team and other members of their business areas.

Management's involvement in the BIA is vital as they provide direction on matters such as the BIA scope and objectives, what constitutes unacceptable losses, criticality levels, and maximum recovery times. The BIA is typically sponsored by one or more members of senior management. A representative from the finance department should be included to help with the analysis of financial impacts.

Management should appoint a project manager to manage and coordinate BIA activities. In some cases, external business continuity consultants provide assistance with the BIA. If external consultants are involved, the project manager should ensure that they work closely with the internal BIA team.

3.5 Methods for Gathering BIA Information

The BIA process relies on the assistance of knowledgeable staff to provide the information related to processes and resources that support their areas of business. Gathering the information needed in the BIA from all relevant areas of the organization can be a complex and challenging task. A structured method is recommended to simplify this task. There are three basic methods available: survey, interview, and workshop.

- **Survey**
  This method uses a set of questions which are sent to each business unit representative. It is accompanied by a cover letter from the business continuity sponsor outlining the reasons for the survey, contact information, and time frame in which the survey should be returned.

  The survey method allows respondents the flexibility to complete the questions at their convenience. There are two main drawbacks of this method. First, the accuracy of responses becomes an issue in the event that the survey questions are misunderstood. Second, the survey responses may not be returned within the time allowed, causing a delay in the overall BIA project schedule.

- **Interview**
  In this method, the BIA information is collected by personally interviewing one or more people. Detailed BIA information can be obtained by tailoring questions for each interview according to the interviewees' areas of expertise. The direct interaction between the interviewees and the interviewer minimizes the possibility of misinterpreting questions. This method is generally more costly than the survey method because of the additional effort needed for planning, scheduling, and conducting interviews.

- **Workshop**

  The workshop method allows a group of people to work collectively to provide the BIA information. Workshop participants discuss both questions and responses to ensure that the BIA information is complete and accurate. Because of the group participation, a workshop generates a large amount of data in a short period of time. A workshop also provides an opportunity to resolve any conflicting BIA information. These advantages outweigh the challenges of bringing appropriate workshop participants together at the same time.

Cost, efficiency, and information quality are some of the factors that influence the choice of a survey, interview, or workshop as a method for gathering BIA information. Usually, more than one method is used in combination to achieve better results. For example, a survey can be sent out to the participants prior to a workshop, allowing them to prepare for the workshop by becoming familiar with the survey questions.

3.6 Recovery Time Requirements

Recovery time requirements consist of several components. Collectively, these components refer to the length of time available to recover from a disruption. An understanding of these components is a prerequisite for conducting the BIA. This section introduces different components of recovery time requirements such as Maximum Tolerable Downtime (MTD), Recovery Time Objective (RTO), Recovery Point Objective (RPO), and Work Recovery Time (WRT).

MTD represents the maximum downtime the organization can tolerate for a business process. RTO indicates the time available to recover disrupted systems/resources. RPO refers to the extent of data loss measured in terms of a time period that can be tolerated by a business process. WRT is the time available to recover the lost data, work backlog, and manually captured data once the systems/resources are recovered or repaired.

MTD, RTO, RPO, and WRT are depicted in Figure 3-1 in the context of a time frame relative to a disruptive event.

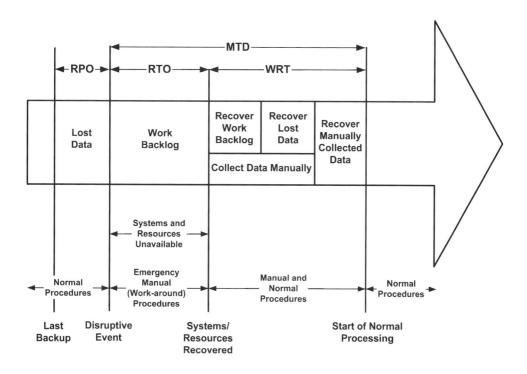

Figure 3-1: Disaster-recovery time frame

The components of recovery time requirements are defined in the context
of three main events:

- **Last Backup of Data**
  This event represents the time the data was last backed up to a
  secure off-site storage facility prior to the disruption.

- **Systems/Resources Recovered**
  This represents the time at which the disrupted systems and resources are replaced or restored to normal conditions.

- **Start of Normal Processing**
  This indicates the time when normal processing of operations can
  begin using the recovered systems.

Events on the time line occur in the following sequence: last backup, disruptive event, systems recovered, and start of normal processing. The time
period between these events are characterized below:

- **Time Period: Last Backup and Disruptive Event**
  The normal procedures in this time period last until the occurrence
  of a disruptive event. The last backup of data to an off-site storage
  facility occurs during the normal procedures. The data processed
  between the time of the last backup and the disruptive event is lost
  because it is not backed up to an off-site storage facility.

- **Time Period: Disruptive Event and Systems/Resources Recovered**
  Following the disruptive event, emergency manual procedures are
  implemented until the systems/resources are recovered. The work
  processed using these manual procedures is considered as "work
  backlog" which will be re-entered or processed later through the
  recovered systems.

- **Time Period: Systems/Resources Recovered and Start of Normal Processing**
  Once the systems/resources are recovered, both manual procedures and normal procedures are implemented concurrently until normal processing can begin. Any new data is recorded or processed manually while the lost data and work backlog is entered or processed through the recovered systems. Next, data collected manually is processed through the recovered systems. Normal processing of data begins after manually collected data is processed.

These time periods help to define the MTD, RTO, RPO, and WRT components of the recovery time requirements, as shown in Figure 3-1. Maximum Tolerable Downtime or MTD is the length of time a process can be unavailable before the company experiences significant losses. MTD corresponds to the time period between a disruptive event and the start of normal processing.

Recovery Time Objective or RTO is associated with the recovery of resources such as computer systems, manufacturing equipment, communication equipment, facilities, etc. RTO is the length of time between a disruptive event and the recovery of systems/resources; it indicates the time available to recover disrupted systems/resources.

Recovery Point Objective or RPO refers to the tolerance for the loss of data measured in terms of the time between the last backup of data and the disaster event. RPO is an indicator of how much lost data can be recovered once systems are recovered and updated with the last backup of data.

Work Recovery Time or WRT is measured as the time between the systems/resource recovery and the start of normal processing. WRT indicates the time needed to recover the lost data, work backlog, and manually captured data once the systems/resources are recovered/repaired.

3.7 BIA's Functional Overview

Conceptually, the BIA process can be described as an activity that takes, as initial input, information related to business processes and produces, as output, information representing an assessment of the impact of a business disruption. A business process is defined as one or more related tasks or activities of a business function. Figure 3-2 provides a functional overview of the BIA process.

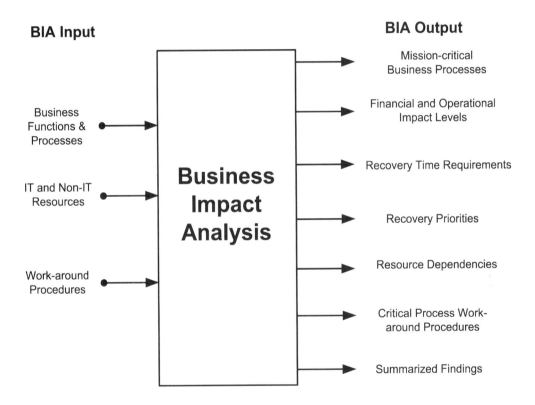

Figure 3-2: BIA input and output information

The initial input to the BIA process includes information regarding business functions and their processes:

- **Business Functions and Processes**
  List of business functions and their processes.

- **IT and Non-IT Resources**
  List of IT and Non-IT resources that support each business process.

- **Work-around Procedures**
  List of work-around procedures that support each business process in the event its normal operation is disrupted.

The output of the BIA process includes the following information:

- **Mission-critical Business Processes**
  These are business processes whose interruption adversely impacts the organization's mission, goals, and objectives.

- **Financial and Operational Impact Levels**
  These levels represent the relative ratings of financial and operational consequences of disrupted business processes.

- **Recovery Time Requirements**
  These are recovery related time requirements for critical processes expressed as Maximum Tolerable Downtime (MTD), Recovery Time Objective (RTO), Recovery Point Objective (RPO), and Work Recovery Time (WRT).

- **Recovery Priorities**
  These represent the sequence for recovering critical processes.

- **Resource Dependencies**
  Resource dependencies are characterized as a list of IT and non-IT resources required by a critical process to perform its normal operation.

- **Critical Process Work-around Procedures**
  Work-around procedures consist of manual or alternative activities that support critical processes in the event their normal operations are interrupted.

- **Summarized Findings**
  These findings provide additional insight regarding the above output of the BIA in a summarized form. Examples of such findings can include expected loss of revenue per day, number of critical processes that need to be recovered within 24 hours, 48 hours, and 72 hours, etc.

3.8 BIA Process

The BIA process consists of a sequence of steps that interact together to identify the impacts of a business disruption and determine the requirements to restore disrupted critical business processes. As shown in Figure 3-3, there are eleven main steps in the BIA process:

Step 1: Define BIA Objectives, Scope, and Assumptions
Step 2: Identify Business Functions and Processes
Step 3: Assess Financial and Operational Impacts
Step 4: Identify Critical Processes
Step 5: Assess MTDs and Prioritize Critical Processes
Step 6: Identify Critical IT Systems and Applications
Step 7: Identify Critical Non-IT Resources

Step 8:   Determine RTO
Step 9:   Determine RPO
Step 10: Identity Work-around Procedures
Step 11: Generate BIA Information Summary

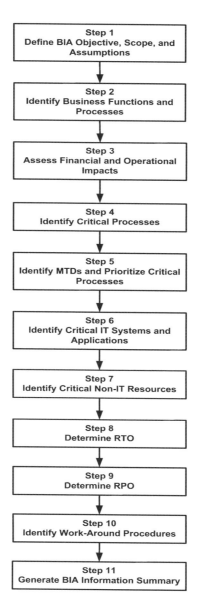

Figure 3-3: BIA process steps

Figure 3-4 shows the information analyzed and produced by various steps
of the BIA process. The rest of this section explains the analysis and
results of each step.

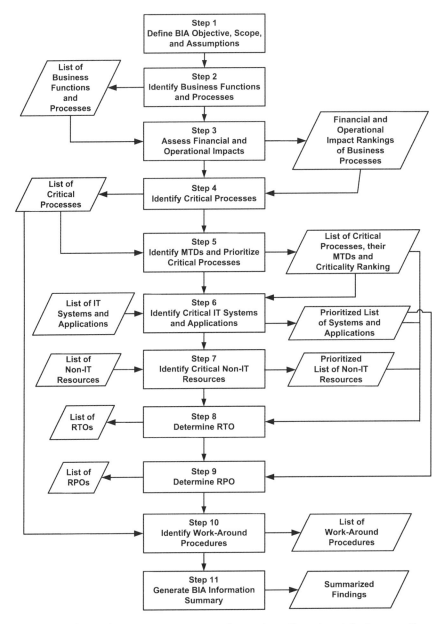

Figure 3-4: BIA process steps – input and output information

3.8.1 Step 1: BIA Objectives, Scope, and Assumptions

This step identifies the objectives, scope, and assumptions needed to guide the BIA process. It provides a basis for

- understanding management's expectations regarding the findings of the BIA,
- defining focus for BIA activities, and
- estimating resources, time, and effort required to conduct the BIA.

The primary objective of the BIA is to identify the impact of business disruption and determine the recovery requirements. The objective of the BIA should also emphasize specific goals and expectations of management regarding its outcome. The following are examples of management goals and expectations:

- Identify mission-critical areas of the business
- Identify potential financial impacts of business disruption
- Identify the gaps in the current recovery capabilities of the organization
- Use the results of the BIA to estimate the business continuity planning budget

The scope helps to focus the BIA effort to certain areas of the organization. For instance, the BIA scope may define the areas of focus to be one or more of

- company-wide,
- specific company sites,
- business functions that are supported by IT systems, or
- business functions that are supported by both IT and non-IT systems and resources.

In addition to the objectives and scope, the initial step of the BIA process specifies certain assumptions that characterize the potential disruptive events and the organization's recovery capabilities. These assumptions become the basis for gathering information related to potential business impacts. Examples of BIA assumptions are given below:

- The disruption occurs during peak processing times.
- There is no alternate IT recovery facility.
- There is no alternate office work area.
- There is no alternate manufacturing and production facility.
- The damaged site becomes inaccessible after the disruption.
- The damaged site becomes functional after a certain pre-established period of time.

3.8.2 Step 2: Identify Business Functions and Processes

The objective of this step is to identify business functions and processes that are used to support the company's mission, goals, and objectives. Sales, customer service, and shipping are a few examples of business functions. Business processes represent the tasks and activities that support the business functions. Table 3-1 lists some examples of business functions and their processes.

Business Function	Business Process
Sales	Generate Orders
	Report Sales Data
Marketing	Promote Products
	Maintain Catalog
Customer Service	Handle Customer Problems
	Process Orders
Shipping	Package Product
	Ship Product

Table 3-1: Example business functions and processes

The scope of the BIA serves as a starting point in the identification of business functions that are analyzed during the BIA process. The company may already have a business model or an organization chart that can assist with the identification of business functions that are within the scope of the BIA. Personnel supporting each business function can identify processes associated with that function, based on their day-to-day tasks and activities. This step results in a list of business functions and processes that become the focus of analysis in other steps of the BIA.

3.8.3 Step 3: Assess Financial and Operational Impacts

This step assesses the financial and operational impacts to the organization in the event of a disruption to the business functions and processes identified in the preceding step. This assessment is based on the BIA assumptions and can be performed as two separate tasks: financial impact assessment and operational impact assessment.

Financial Impact Assessment

Financial impacts measure the extent and severity of financial loss to the business. The assessment of the financial impact is performed for each business process by asking the question "What would be the extent and severity of financial loss if the process were interrupted following a disaster?" The question is asked in the context of the assumptions which characterize the disruptive event, as specified in Step 1.

The first part of the financial impact assessment is to determine the extent of probable monetary losses following a disruptive event. It is useful to estimate the amount of these monetary losses over a fixed period of time in order to facilitate a comparison of financial impacts associated with different processes. This part of the assessment considers various causes of lost revenue and extra expenses that may occur from the disruption.

A common cause of monetary loss is lost sales of products and services, but it may also be attributed to other factors, such as

- penalties due to contractual obligations,
- lost funding,
- loss of discounts, and
- lost opportunities to earn interest.

Extra expenses also have financial impacts. Examples of these expenses are costs associated with

- acquiring temporary employees to help with recovery tasks;
- travel, accommodation, and lodging;
- overtime wages for additional work;
- shipping systems and equipment; and
- replacement equipment rental.

Table 3-2 lists examples of the rate of financial loss per day for business processes of Table 3-1.

Business Function	Business Process	Extent of Financial Loss (per day)
Sales	Generate Orders	$700,000
	Report Sales Data	$0
Marketing	Promote Products	$10,000
	Maintain Catalog	$5,000
Customer Service	Handle Customer Problems	$5,000
	Process Orders	$500,000
Shipping	Package Product	$15,000
	Ship Product	$20,000

Table 3-2: Example of financial impacts

The second part of the financial impact assessment ranks each impact on a severity level based on its monetary loss value. The following are example severity levels ranging from "no impact" to "major impact":

1. Severity level 0 (no impact)
2. Severity level 1 (minor impact)
3. Severity level 2 (intermediate impact)
4. Severity level 3 (major impact)

Examples of severity levels for financial impacts of Table 3-2 are listed in Table 3-3.

Business Function	Business Process	Extent of Financial Loss (per day)	Severity Level
Sales	Generate Orders	$700,000	3
	Report Sales Data	$0	0
Marketing	Promote Products	$2,000	1
	Maintain Catalog	$5,000	1
Customer Service	Handle Customer Problems	$5000	1
	Process Orders	$500,000	3
Shipping	Package Product	$15,000	2
	Ship Product	$20,000	2

Table 3-3: Example of financial impacts and severity levels

Operational Impact Assessment

The operational impact assessment measures the negative impact of a disruptive event on various aspects of business operations related to adequacy, efficiency, satisfaction, image, confidence, control, morale, etc.

The following are examples of operational impacts:

- Inadequate cash flow
- Loss of investor confidence
- Loss of market share
- Loss of competitive edge
- Damage to shareholder confidence
- Damage to industry reputation
- Low staff morale
- Unsatisfactory customer service
- Damage to vendor relations
- Violation of regulatory controls

The operational impact rankings that are assigned to business processes represent subjective estimates, provided by BIA participants who are most knowledgeable about business processes and potential impacts.

The operational impacts can be measured using a quantitative ranking scheme such as low, medium, high, highest, and none. For instance, if the impact to a business process from an operational aspect is considered significant, a ranking of a "high" value may be assigned to that process.

Example operational impact rankings for processes of Table 3-1 are given in Table 3-4.

Business Function	Business Process	Operational Impacts Ranking				
		Cash Flow	Investor Confidence	Market Share	Competitive Edge	Customer Satisfaction
Sales	Generate Orders	high	high	highest	high	none
	Report Sales Data	none	highest	low	none	none
Marketing	Promote Products	low	high	high	highest	low
	Maintain Catalog	low	medium	high	highest	high
Customer Service	Handle Customer Problems	medium	low	low	medium	high
	Process Orders	highest	medium	low	medium	highest
Shipping	Package Product	high	medium	low	high	high
	Ship Product	high	medium	low	high	high

Table 3-4: Example of operational impact ratings

The rankings in the above table focus on five different operational aspects: cash flow, investor confidence, market share, competitive edge, and customer satisfaction. The rankings for a business process represent the level of negative impact in the event it is disrupted. For example, disruption to the "Maintain Catalog" process is expected to have a significant (high) negative impact to both market share and customer satisfaction; an extremely significant (highest) negative impact to competitive edge; an insignificant (low) impact on cash flow; and a medium impact on investor confidence.

3.8.4 Step 4: Identify Critical Business Processes

This step identifies business processes that are critical for maintaining business continuity. The financial and operational impact rankings assigned in Step 3 provide a basis for identifying critical business processes. Selection criteria are established to determine whether a given process qualifies as "critical". An example of selection criteria is given below.

A process is considered critical if any one of the following is true:

1   A severity level of 2 or 3 is assigned to its financial impact.
2   A ranking of "high" is assigned to at least three of its operational impacts.
3   A ranking of "high" is assigned to at least two and a ranking of "highest" is assigned to at least one of its operational aspects.
4   A ranking of "highest" is assigned to at least two of its operational impacts.

The critical processes listed in Table 3-5 are obtained by applying the above selection criteria to the impact rankings of business processes in Table 3-3 and Table 3-4.

Critical Business Function	Critical Business Process
Sales	Generate Orders
Marketing	Promote Products
	Maintain Catalog
Customer Service	Process Orders
Shipping	Package Product
	Ship Products

Table 3-5: Critical business processes

3.8.5 Step 5: Identify MTDs and Prioritize Critical Processes

Once the critical business processes are known, the BIA process identifies their Maximum Tolerable Downtimes (MTD) and prioritizes them according to their recovery priorities. MTD is the length of time a process can remain unavailable before the financial and operational impacts reach an unacceptable level. Estimates of MTD can be based on either financial impacts or operational impacts.

As an example of how financial impacts are used to estimate MTD, consider the business process "Generate Orders" in Table 3-3 and Table 3-4. This process is identified as having a financial impact severity level of 3, and operational impact values that are either "high" or "highest" with respect to cash flow, investor confidence, market share, and competitive edge.

The BIA participants responsible for assessing the financial and operational impacts are asked the question "What is the maximum period of time that can be tolerated for this process based on the financial and operational impact levels?" Assume that a financial loss of $7,000 per day becomes unacceptable when it exceeds $21,000 in three days. Therefore, the MTD is three days since the financial losses will exceed $21,000 if the disruption continues longer. This example assumes that the operational impacts are insignificant relative to the financial losses.

An example of how operational impacts are used to estimate MTD, consider the business process, "Promote Products". The MTD for this process is estimated as seven days according to the BIA. The estimate is based on the premise that a disruption of more than seven days can cause an unacceptable level of damage to investor confidence, competitive edge, and market share.

Given the MTDs of critical business processes, a priority for their recovery can be established. A critical business process that has a shorter MTD compared with another critical process is assigned a higher recovery priority. Table 3-6 shows example MTDs and recovery priorities for the critical business processes of Table 3-5.

Critical Business Function	Critical Business Process	MTD	Recovery Priority
Sales	Generate Orders	3 days	1
	Report Sales Data	5 days	2
Marketing	Promote Products	7 days	4
	Maintain Catalog	5 days	3
Customer Service	Process Orders	3 days	1
Shipping	Package Product	4 days	2
	Ship Product	4 days	2

Table 3-6: MTDs and recovery priorities

3.8.6 Step 6: Identify Critical IT Systems and Applications

An IT system or an application is considered "critical" if it supports a critical business process. This step identifies critical IT systems and applications that support processes identified in Step 4.

The first task in this step is to compile a list of all systems and applications used by the business. Ideally, the IT department within the company should assist with compiling this list. The next task is to map each critical business process to the systems and applications which support them.

Both the IT department and the business process owners should help with this mapping task. Table 3-7 maps the processes of Table 3-5 to example systems and applications.

Critical Business Function	Critical Business Process	Critical IT Systems and Applications
Sales	Generate Orders	Customer Information System
		Order Entry System
		E-mail application
		EDI application
		Sales Inquiry Tracking System
Marketing	Promote Products	Customer Information System
		E-mail application
	Maintain Catalog	On-line Catalog Application
Customer Service	Process Orders	Order Entry System
		Inventory Management System
		Customer Billing System
Shipping	Package Product	Order Entry System
		Shipping and Freight Management System
	Ship Product	Shipping and Freight Management System
		Inventory Management System
		Order Entry System

Table 3-7: A mapping of critical business processes to critical IT systems and applications

The following is a description of example critical IT systems and applications listed in Table 3-7.

- **Customer Information System:** This system maintains customer information such as company name, contact information, mailing address, shipping address, credit history, etc. It is used primarily by the sales and marketing departments. This application interfaces with the Order Entry System and Sales Inquiry Tracking System.

- **Order Entry System:** This system is used to enter, process, and track customer orders. It is used by sales, customer service, and shipping departments.

- **EDI Application:** EDI (Electronic Data Interchange) application is used to receive a customer's order through computer-to-computer electronic exchange of documents. This application interfaces with the Order Entry System.

- **Sales Inquiry Tracking System:** This system is used by the sales department to keep track of information related to potential sales opportunities. It maintains sales inquiry information such as contact name, company name and address, inquiry date and time, and potential sales orders and revenues, etc. This system interfaces with the Customer Information System and Order Entry System.

- **On-line Catalog Application:** This is a web-based catalog application that customers can use to obtain product information through the Internet.

- **Customer Billing System:** This system manages customer invoicing, account receivables, credit control, pricing, and payment processing, etc. It is integrated with the financial institutions to process customers' electronic payments. It interfaces with the Order Entry System and Shipping and Freight Management System.

- **Shipping and Freight Management System:** This system manages the key functions needed for shipping products to customers, such as shipment scheduling, weighing, labeling, tracking, and rating. This system interfaces with the Customer Billing System and Inventory Management System.

- **Inventory Management System:** This system maintains, tracks, and controls inventory. Every item in the inventory is tracked from the time it is received, from the supplier, to the time it is shipped to the customer. This system interfaces with the Shipping and Freight Management System and Order Entry System.

- **E-mail Application:** This application is used by the entire organization for internal and external communication.

3.8.7 Step 7: Critical Non-IT Resources

Non-IT resources are used throughout the organization to support various functions and services. Below are examples of different types of non-IT resources:

- IT facility and manufacturing and production facility
- Office work area
- Manufacturing and production equipment
- Raw material
- Office furniture
- Safety equipment
- Voice communication equipment
- Maintenance tools and supplies
- Critical records
- Fax, printing, and copying equipment
- Office stationery

This step identifies critical non-IT resources that are required by the critical business processes. The business process owners should assist with compiling a list of non-IT resources that are essential for their business process.

Tables 3-8, 3-9, and 3-10 list examples of non-IT resources for critical business processes shown in Table 3-5. Table 3-8 lists critical manufacturing and production resources for the "Package Product" process. Table 3-9 lists the critical office work area non-IT resources for the "Generate Orders" process. Table 3-10 details the office work area facility requirements of the staff to perform the "Generate Orders", "Promote Products", "Maintain Catalog", and "Process Orders" processes.

Critical Business Function	Critical Business Process	Critical Manufacturing and Production Resources	
		Resource Type	Resource Details
Shipping	Package Product	Machinery/ Equipment	Horizontal case packer
		Raw material	Corrugated boxes Sealing materials: • Hot melt glue • Tape • Cold glue Cushioning materials: • White Polyethylene Foam Rolls • White Polyethylene Foam Rolls in Dispenser Box • Anti-Static Polyethylene Foam Rolls in Dispenser Box • Poly Foam Bags • Convoluted Foam Sheets • Anti-Static Polystyrene Loose Fill
		Tools	Forklift; Case packing machinery repair tools.
		Furniture	Desk and chairs for supervisor; A general purpose long desk and chairs. Lunch room furniture.
		Safety equipment	Hard safety hats, safety gloves.
		Voice communication equipment	3 phones with voice mail, call waiting, and call forwarding options.
		Maintenance Supplies	Machine oil, filters, etc.
		Critical records	Packaging equipment operation manual; safety guideline document.

Table 3-8: Critical manufacturing and production resources for "Package Product" process

Critical Business Function	Critical Business Process	Critical Office Work Area Resources	
		Resource Type	Resource Details
Sales	Generate Orders	Voice Communication Equipment	8 phones with voice mail, call waiting, and call forwarding options.
		Fax	2 faxes; 1 for sending and 1 for receiving faxes.
		Printer	1 laser printer.
		Copier	1 high speed copier.
		Stationery	Paper pads, pens, binders, staplers, printing and copying paper, etc.
		Critical Records	Order forms; Product list; Pricing list; and Customer list; fax cover page; letter heads.
		Office Furniture	8 cubicles with desks and chairs; 1 table and 15 chairs and a white board for a meeting room.

Table 3-9: Critical office work area resources for "Generate Orders" process

Critical Business Processes	Office Work Area Facility
Generate Orders, Promote Products, Maintain Catalog, Process Orders.	Floor area of 3000 square feet
	Parking spaces for 15 cars
	Air conditioning, heating, and ventilation systems.
	Smoke and carbon-monoxide detectors, Emergency exit lights, fire alarms, and sprinkler system.
	Washroom facility for 50 staff
	Security controlled facility
	Loading dock

Table 3-10: Critical office work area facility

3.8.8 Step 8: Determine Recovery Time Objective (RTO)

Recovery Time Objective or RTO, as depicted in Figure 3-1, is associated with the recovery of disrupted IT and non-IT resources such as computer systems, manufacturing equipment, communication equipment, and facilities. RTO is the length of time between a disaster event and recovery of resources; it indicates the time available to recover disrupted resources.

The information from steps 5, 6, and 7 are used to determine the RTO for each non-IT and IT resource. The MTD value obtained from Step 5 expresses the maximum limit for the RTO value. The MTD consists of both RTO and Work Recovery Time (WRT). WRT is the time needed to complete the disrupted work on a recovered/repaired resource in order to return it to normal status. For IT systems, WRT represents the time needed to recover lost data and enter work backlog and manually collected data.

Table 3-11 lists examples of RTO and WRT values for "Generate Orders" process. According to these RTO and WRT values, the "Generate Orders"

Critical Business Function	Critical Business Process	Critical IT Systems and Applications	RTO	WRT
Sales	Generate Orders	Customer Information System	2.5 days	0.5 day
		Order Entry System	1 day	2 days
		E-mail application	2.5 days	0.5 day
		EDI application	2 days	1 day
		Sales Inquiry Tracking System	2.8 days	0.2 day

Table 3-11: RTO and WRT for IT systems that support "Generate Orders" process

process has an MTD of three days. The IT systems and applications that support this process need to be recovered earlier than three days in order to accommodate both the RTO and WRT. The Order Entry System has the least RTO value of one day and a WRT value of two days.

3.8.9 Step 9: Determine Recovery Point Objective (RPO)

RPO expresses the tolerance to a loss of data as a result of a disruptive event. It is measured as the time between the last data backup and the disruptive event, as shown in Figure 3-1.

As an example of how RPO is determined, consider an electric utility company's system that supports an application to track customers' power consumption. The application is assigned an RPO of 48 hours with a backup of data occurring once every 48 hours. This value of RPO indicates that the company can tolerate a loss of data for up to 48 hours in the event of a system disruption. The tolerance of 48 hours is attributed to the data capacity of hand-held meter reading equipment which the company uses to read customers' power consumption. The hand-held meter reader can store collected data for up to 48 hours. In the event of a disaster, the system can be recovered by first restoring the data from the last 48 hour backup, followed by the data stored in the hand-held meter reading equipment.

The BIA determines RPO for each application by asking participants the question "What is the tolerance, in terms of length of time, to loss of data that may occur between any two backup periods?" The response to this question indicates the values of Recovery Point Objectives.

3.8.10 Step 10: Identify Work-Around Procedures

Work-around procedures allow business processes to continue, in the event that IT and non-IT resources are unavailable, through alternative methods. The alternative methods, which often involve manual operations, tend to be temporary, less efficient, or more expensive compared with normal procedures. This step identifies work-around procedures for business processes selected as critical in Step 4.

The BIA identifies information regarding work-around procedures for each critical business process, in the event that resources are unavailable, by asking participants the following questions:

- "Are there any documented work-around procedures that exist for your process?"
- "Identify any work which is not covered by these work-around procedures?"

Table 3-12 provides examples of work-around procedures for the "Generate Orders" and "Package Product" processes.

Critical Business Function	Critical Business Process	Critical IT Systems and Applications	Work-Around Procedures
Sales	Generate Orders	Order Entry System	Manually track customer orders using customer information on Microfiche records. Manually process orders with the exception of financial credit approval. Process financial credit approval through the once the system is recovered and the external credit check link is established.
Shipping	Package Product	Machinery Equipment: Horizontal Case Packer	Manually package products for small and medium boxes only. Package large boxes once the packaging equipment is operational.

Table 3-12: Examples of work-around procedures for IT and non-IT resources

3.8.11 Step 11: Generate BIA Information Summary

The results of preceding steps are summarized in this step to provide additional insight into the overall findings of the BIA. The summarized findings, for example, can provide the following information:

- Ratio of the number of business processes to the number of critical business processes per business function
- Average value of RTO for all critical business processes

- Average value of MTD for all critical business processes
- Expected financial loss per day of business interruption

3.9 BIA Report

At the end of the BIA process a report is generated that includes two types of information:

- Details of the key outputs from the steps of the BIA process
- Summarized findings of Step 11

The output information of the BIA process is shown in Figure 3-4. Below is a recommended set of outputs of the BIA that should be part of the report:

- List of critical processes from Step 4
- List of MTDs and criticality rankings from Step 5
- Prioritized list of systems and applications from Step 6
- Prioritized list of non-IT resources from Step 7
- List of RTOs from Step 8
- List of RPOs from Step 9
- List of work-around procedures from Step 10

Chapter 4
Business Continuity Strategy Development

4.1 Chapter Overview

The objective of the third stage of the BCP process (see Figure 1-3) is to develop a business continuity strategy that satisfies the business recovery requirements identified in the BIA stage. The business continuity strategy is composed of a set of recovery options to be utilized as alternatives in the event that existing critical resources become unavailable. Business recovery requirements can generally be grouped into four recovery areas:

- Work areas
- IT systems and infrastructure
- Manufacturing and production
- Data and critical/vital records

Below are examples of recovery requirements for these areas:

- Work areas:
  - Arrange an alternate work area for the crisis management team
  - Arrange an alternate office work area for staff

- IT systems and infrastructure:
  - Arrange an alternate facility for recovering IT systems
  - Recover damaged systems

- Manufacturing and production:
  - Recover damaged manufacturing equipment

- Data and critical/vital records:
  - Restore damaged critical records
  - Restore lost data

Table 4-1 lists examples of recovery options for the above requirements.

Recovery Requirement	Recovery Option
Crisis management team needs an alternate work area.	Book a hotel meeting room after a disaster event to be used as a crisis management center.
Staff needs a work area.	Prior to a disaster, establish a contract with a vendor for a mobile site to be delivered to a specified location within an agreed time. The mobile site is to be used by staff as an alternate work facility.
An alternate facility is required for recovering IT systems.	Establish a contract, prior to a disaster, for a hot site complete with installed systems and infrastructure to be used as an alternate IT recovery facility.
Recover damaged manufacturing equipment.	Maintain a surplus of critical parts at a remote site to repair damaged manufacturing equipment.
Restore damaged critical records.	Acquire a vendor to salvage and restore damaged critical records.
Recover damaged systems.	Make arrangements with a vendor to quick-ship damaged systems within an agreed time frame.
Restore lost data.	Ensure that data is backed-up daily at an off-site storage facility.

Table 4-1: Example recovery requirements and recovery options

This chapter describes a framework for developing the business continuity strategy. The framework begins by identifying business recovery requirements, and ends with a set of recovery options for the business continuity strategy. Within the framework, several recovery options are considered as possible solutions to address the recovery requirements. For instance, in the area of IT systems and infrastructure, potential recovery options include a hot site, cold site, or warm site. These options generally have different recovery times, costs, and capabilities associated with them. Only those options that meet the recovery time requirements are selected for further assessment. The final assessment in the framework compares costs and capabilities of the selected options and determines the most appropriate and viable option.

This chapter also describes general business continuity strategy considerations and strategy related recommendations for recovery contracts and agreements.

4.2 A Framework for BC Strategy Development

The business continuity strategy development framework consists of four phases:

- Phase A: Recovery Requirements Identification
- Phase B: Recovery Options Identification
- Phase C: Availability Time Assessment
- Phase D: Cost-Capability Assessment

Phase A of the framework determines the recovery requirements to be addressed by the business continuity strategy. Phase B identifies possible options as solutions to the recovery requirements. Phase C eliminates those options that do not meet the recovery time requirements. With the remaining options, Phase D assesses their cost and capability trade-offs to select the most viable and effective option.

Figure 4-1 illustrates the four phases of the business continuity strategy development framework. Phases A through D are described in greater details in the Sections 4.2.1 to 4.2.4.

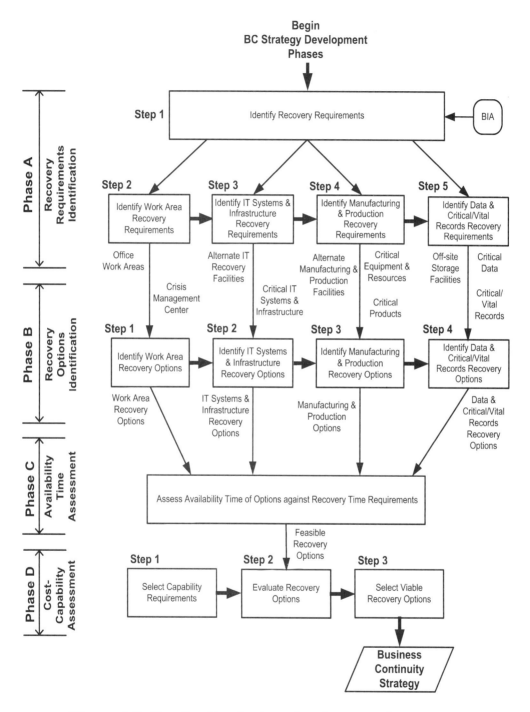

Figure 4-1: Continuity strategy development framework

4.2.1 Phase A: Recovery Requirements Identification

Phase A identifies the recovery requirements to be addressed by the business continuity strategy. Phase A consists of five steps as shown in Figure 4-1. Step 1 produces a list of recovery requirements to be addressed by the business continuity strategy. These requirements, which are primarily derived from the BIA, identify

- critical business processes and resources that should be the focus of the recovery strategy, and
- time requirements (MTD, WRT, RTO, RPO) for recovering these processes and resources.

Step 1 can also produce additional recovery requirements not included in the BIA. Examples of such additional requirements are the resources needed to support the crisis management center, a facility from which the crisis management team directs recovery efforts. The center can be located in an office work area or a hotel conference room. For more information on crisis management center activities see Chapter 5 *Business Continuity Plan Development*.

Steps 2 to 5 of this phase groups the recovery requirements, identified in Step 1, into different recovery areas. Four common recovery areas are

- Work areas,
- IT systems and infrastructure,
- Manufacturing and production, and
- Data and critical/vital records.

The recovery requirements for each recovery area are further divided into different categories. Steps 2 to 5 produce detailed requirements for each category corresponding to their recovery area. The list below shows the recovery areas and requirement categories for steps 2 to 5:

- **Step 2**

    Recovery Area: Work areas

    Recovery Requirement Categories:
    a) Alternate office work areas, for staff to perform work
    b) Crisis management center, for crisis management team to conduct recovery efforts

- **Step 3**

    Recovery Area: IT systems and infrastructure

    Recovery Requirement Categories:
    a) Critical IT systems and infrastructure
    b) Alternate IT recovery facilities

- **Step 4**

    Recovery Area: Manufacturing and production

    Recovery Requirement Categories:
    a) Critical equipment and resources
    b) Critical products
    c) Alternate manufacturing and production facilities

- **Step 5**

    Recovery Area: Data and critical/vital records

    Recovery Requirement Categories:
    a) Critical data[1] and off-site data storage facilities
    b) Critical records and off-site record storage facilities

The recovery requirements from Phase A are assessed in phases B, C, and D described in sections 4.2.2, 4.2.3, and 4.2.4.

---

[1] Critical data can include critical IT applications and components needed to support those applications, such as operating systems, databases, and data.

4.2.2 Phase B: Recovery Options Identification

The objective of Phase B is to identify available recovery options for the recovery requirements produced in Phase A. As depicted in Figure 4-1, this phase is divided into four steps, each assigned to a specific recovery area. These steps identify recovery options available for the requirements related to their recovery areas. For example, Step 1 identifies three options available for recovering IT systems and infrastructure:

1. **Pre-established**—where systems are acquired and installed prior to a disruptive event and are used only for recovery purposes.
2. **Pre-arranged (quick-ship)**—where an agreement is made with a vendor that guarantees the delivery of the required systems within an agreed time following a disruptive event.
3. **Acquire-as-needed**—where the required systems are ordered from a supplier following a disruptive event.

Tables 4-2 to 4-9 are examples of recovery options available for the recovery areas assigned to steps 1 to 4. Each table lists recovery options and their descriptions and categories. The following list shows how the recovery options relate to the steps and recovery areas:

- **Phase B Step 1**
  Recovery Area: Work areas
  Recovery Requirement Category:
    a) Alternate office work areas
    b) Crisis management center
  Recovery Options:
    See Table 4-2: Recovery options for alternate office work areas and crisis management center

- **Phase B Step 2**

  Recovery Area: IT systems and infrastructure

  Recovery Requirement Category:
  a) Critical IT systems and infrastructure
  b) Alternate IT recovery facilities

  Recovery Options:
  a) See Table 4-3: Recovery options for critical IT systems and infrastructure
  b) See Table 4-4: Recovery options for alternate IT recovery facilities

- **Phase B Step 3**

  Recovery Area: Manufacturing and production

  Recovery Requirement Category:
  a) Critical equipment and resources
  b) Critical products
  c) Alternate manufacturing and production facilities

  Recovery Options:
  a) See Table 4-5: Recovery options for critical equipment and resources
  b) See Table 4-6: Recovery options for critical products
  c) See Table 4-7: Recovery options for alternate manufacturing and production   facilities

- **Phase B Step 4**

  Recovery Area: Critical data and critical/vital records

  Recovery Requirement Category:
  a) Critical data and off-site data storage facilities
  b) Critical records and off-site record storage facilities

  Recovery Options:
  a) See Table 4-8: Recovery options for critical data and off-site data storage facilities
  b) See Table 4-9: Recovery options for critical records and off-site record storage facilities

Recovery Option Category	Recovery Options	Option Description
Commercial	Mobile site	A mobile site is an alternate recovery facility in a vehicle that is delivered to a desired location. It is typically pre-configured with desks, chairs, hardware, software, data and voice communications equipment.
	Hotel meeting rooms	Hotel facilities.
	Fixed site	An alternate recovery facility at a fixed location offered as a service by a vendor. It may have office equipment, communication lines, etc.
Company Owned	Alternate company owned site or branch office	An alternate recovery facility at a fixed company owned location. It may have office equipment, communication lines, etc.
Employee Owned	Home office	Part of an employee's home used as an office.
Critical Resource Acquisition Method	Pre-established	Critical resources are acquired prior to a disaster and used for recovery purposes only.
	Pre-arranged (quick-ship)	An agreement is made with a vendor that guarantees the delivery of the required resources within an agreed time following a disruptive event.
	Acquire-as-needed	The required critical resources are ordered as needed from suppliers following a disruptive event.

Table 4-2: Recovery options for alternate office work areas and crisis management center

Recovery Option Category	Recovery Options	Option Description
System Acquisition Method	Pre-established	The systems are acquired and installed prior to a disruptive event and used for recovery purposes only.
	Pre-arranged (quick-ship)	An agreement is made with a vendor that guarantees the delivery of the required systems within an agreed time following a disruptive event.
	Acquire-as-needed	The required systems are ordered from the supplier following a disruptive event as needed.

Table 4-3: Recovery options for critical IT systems and infrastructure

Recovery Option Category	Recovery Options	Option Description
Ownership	Company owned remote site	An alternate recovery facility at a fixed company-owned location to be used for IT recovery in the event of a disaster.
	Mobile site	A mobile site is an alternate recovery facility in a vehicle that is delivered to a desired location. It is typically pre-configured with desks, chairs, hardware, software, data and voice communications equipment.
	Reciprocal site involving a separate organization	Based on an agreement between two organizations to share each others facilities for recovery purposes in the event of a disaster.
	Commercially available dedicated site	An alternate recovery facility, which is dedicated to a single organization, offered as a service by a vendor.
	Commercially available shared site	An alternate recovery facility, which is shared by multiple organizations, offered as a service by a vendor.
Operational Readiness	Cold site	A cold site is an alternate recovery facility that does not have any hardware, software, or data and voice communication equipment. It may include amenities such as: 1. Power 2. Air-conditioning 3. Heating 4. Water 5. Fire sprinklers 6. Data and voice communication lines 7. Raised floors for computing equipment
	Warm site	A warm site is an alternate recovery facility that has some of the necessary hardware, software, data and voice communication equipment pre-installed. Additional equipment is normally provided within a certain defined time period. A warm site may need to be prepared before receiving equipment.
	Hot site	A hot site is an alternate recovery facility that contains pre-configured hardware, software, data and voice communications equipment.

Table 4-4: Recovery options for alternate IT recovery facilities

Recovery Option Category	Recovery Options	Option Description
Acquire-as-needed	Acquire equipment	The manufacturing equipment is acquired as needed after the disaster occurs.
	Acquire parts	The manufacturing equipment parts are acquired as needed after the disaster occurs.
Pre-established	Maintain contracted services to salvage and restore	A contract/agreement to salvage and restore any damaged equipment and resources is established with a vendor prior to a disruptive event.
	Maintain a backup of critical parts at an off-site facility	A supply of critical parts is stored prior to a disruptive event at an off-site storage facility as a backup.
	Maintain backups of critical equipment at an off-site facility	Critical equipment is stored as backup prior to a disruptive event at an off-site storage facility.

Table 4-5: Recovery options for critical equipment and resources

Recovery Option Category	Recovery Options	Option Description
Backup Supply Inventory	Maintain a supply of raw materials and products needed during recovery time at a remote warehouse.	A supply of products is stored at a remote warehouse prior to a disruptive event.
Production Assistance	Establish reciprocal arrangements with other similar organizations for recovery assistance	A mutual agreement is established with another organization such that one organization can supply products to customers in the event the other one is impacted by a disruptive event.

Table 4-6: Recovery options for critical products

Recovery Option Category	Recovery Options	Option Description
Alternate Recovery Facility	Use company's existing empty facility at another location	An empty alternate company facility at a remote location having minimum facilities such as power, heating, air-conditioning, fire sprinklers, etc.
	Acquire a separate commercially available facility as needed	A commercial facility is acquired for recovery purposes following a disruptive event at the primary site.
	Rebuild or repair the damaged site	The damaged primary site is rebuilt or repaired following a disruptive event.
	Share company's existing secondary manufacturing and production facility	Arrangements are made with another manufacturing facility within the same company to produce products in the event that the primary site is disrupted.

Table 4-7: Recovery options for alternate manufacturing and production facilities

Recovery Option Category	Recovery Options	Option Description
Data Backup Frequency	Continuous	Data is backed up to an off-site storage location on continuous basis using real-time data replication and backup techniques.
	Daily	Data is backed up once every day.
	Weekly	Data is backed up once every week.
	Monthly	Data is backed up once every month.
Backup Type	Full	A full or normal backup of all files.
	Incremental	A backup of only those files created or changed since the last full backup or incremental backup.
	Differential	A backup of only those files created or changed since the last full backup.
Backup Method	Remote Mirroring	Data is mirrored at a alternate recovery facility to provide continuous availability using technology such as transaction routers, and proprietary fault tolerant redundant systems.
	Wide Area High Availability Clustering	This method uses software and hardware based equipment organized as in a wide area network that can be automatically reconfigured to replace a failed machine.
	Storage Area Network (SAN)	High speed high performance network that enables computers with different operating systems to communicate with one storage device.
	Storage Virtualization	Combines multiple storage devices into a logical virtual storage device that can be centrally managed. It is presented as single storage pool.
	Disk Mirroring	A controller on a primary disk writes to a controller on a secondary disk in synchronous mode.
	Disk Shadowing	Changes to the data on a primary disk are continuously captured on a log which is later applied to a secondary server disk in asynchronous mode.
	Application or Utility based data replication	An application or a utility sends primary server data to a secondary off-site application server.
	Electronic Vaulting	Backups created automatically via an electronic vaulting provider.
	Remote Journaling	Transaction logs or journals are sent to an alternate recovery facility.
	Tape backups	Traditional backups using tape media.
Off-site Storage Facility	Commercial data storage facility	Remote storage sites offered by a commercial vendor to store data on backup media. The site is typically secure and environmentally safe.
	Company owned remote data storage facility	Remote storage site within the company where the data is stored on backup media. The site is typically secure and environmentally safe.

Table 4-8: Recovery options for critical data and off-site data storage facilities

Recovery Option Category	Recovery Options	Option Description
Backup Frequency	Daily	Records are backed up once every day.
	Weekly	Records are backed up once every week.
	Monthly	Records are backed up once every month.
	Yearly	Records are backed up once every year.
Storage Media	Microfilm	Different types of media to store the critical records as backups.
	Microfiche	
	Optical disk	
	Magnetic tapes	
	Disks	
	CD	
Salvage and Restore Method	Pre-arranged contract with a vendor for salvage and restore operation	A contract/agreement is established with a vendor to salvage and restore any damaged records prior to a disruptive event.
	Contract on an as-needed basis for salvage and restore	A contract/agreement is established with a vendor to salvage and restore any damaged records following a disruptive event.
Off-site Storage Facility	Commercially operated record storage sites	Remote storage sites offered by a commercial vendor to store records on backup media. The site is typically secure and environmentally safe to protect the stored media.
	Company owned remote record storage site	Remote storage site within the company where the records are stored on backup media. The site is typically secure and environmentally safe to protect the stored media.

Table 4-9: Recovery options for critical records and off-site record storage facilities

4.2.3 Phase C: Availability Time Assessment

The purpose of this phase is to determine the viability of recovery options identified in Phase B through an assessment of Expected Availability Time (EAT) of resources specified in the options. For each option, this assessment involves three main steps:

Step 1:   Evaluate the EAT of the resources
Step 2:   Compare the EAT with the recovery time requirements—
          Maximum Tolerable Downtimes (MTDs), Recovery Time
          Objectives (RTOs), Recovery Point Objectives (RPOs), and
          Work Recovery Times (WRTs)
Step 3:   Select the recovery option as viable if its EAT satisfies the
          recovery time requirements

As an example of this assessment, assume that a pre-arranged (quick-ship) acquisition of IT systems has been selected as a recovery option by Phase A. Also, assume that the MTD, RTO, and WRT are less than ten days. The first step evaluates the EAT for IT systems and determines its value as seven days which allows four days for delivery of IT systems (based on the pre-arranged acquisition option) and three days for system recovery. The second step compares the EAT of seven days with the IT systems recovery requirements of ten days. Step 3 selects this option as viable because the EAT of seven days satisfies the ten-day recovery requirements.

The options selected in Step 3 are used as input to the next phase; the options that were not selected are eliminated.

Step 1 of the assessment requires a detailed evaluation of various concerns or factors that can adversely impact the EAT of resources. Examples of availability time concerns for various options are described in the tables of Appendix 4A "Availability Time Concerns for Recovery Options", at the end of this chapter. The information in these tables is not exhaustive and not all of it will be applicable in every situation.

4.2.4 Phase D: Cost-Capability Assessment

The recovery options that satisfy the recovery time requirements in Phase C are further analyzed and compared in Phase D. The purpose of this analysis and comparison is to select the options which best satisfy the recovery cost and capability requirements. The selected options become part of the business continuity strategy.

As a simple example of this phase, assume that Phase B identified the following two system acquisition options for the recovery of critical IT systems and infrastructure:

—Pre-established
—Pre-arranged (quick-ship)

These two options require further analysis and a comparison of their costs and capabilities. For instance, compared to the pre-arranged (quick-ship) option, the cost of pre-established acquisition of systems is generally higher. The recovery effort with a pre-arranged option, however, is more difficult because the option often requires additional installation and configuration steps compared to the pre-established option. In the pre-established option, such installation and configuration steps occur prior to a disruptive event. Based on this simple comparison, Phase D may select the pre-established system acquisition option if the cost is less of a concern compared with the recovery effort.

There are three main steps in Phase D. Step 1 defines a list of attributes to measure capabilities of recovery options. The capability attributes, which represent specific recovery requirements and preferences of an organization, can include the following:

• Effort—estimates how much effort is needed to implement an option

- Quality—estimates the quality of products, data, and service associated with an option

- Safety—estimates how well an option satisfies safety requirements

- Control—estimates how much control organizations have over the use and implementation of an option

- Security—estimates physical and information security aspects of an option

Step 2 of phase D evaluates each option in order to determine its cost and assign values to its capability attributes. Qualitative metrics such as low, medium, or high can be assigned to both cost and capability attributes—a low value indicates that an option has a high cost or less capability, while a high value represents a low cost or high capability.

Table 4-10 shows an example assignment of values (ratings) to cost and capability attributes of the following recovery options for the IT systems and infrastructure recovery area:

IT System and Infrastructure Acquisition Options
1. Pre-established
2. Pre-arranged (quick-ship)

Alternate IT Recovery Facility Options
1. Company owned cold site
2. Commercial hot site

The final step, Step 3, selects the most appropriate option by comparing their relative costs and capabilities. The discussion below explains the selection process for the example options in Table 4-10.

	Options	Recovery Effort	Quality	Safety	Control	Security	Cost
1	Pre-established	Low	High	Not applicable	High	Not applicable	High
2	Pre-arranged (quick-ship)	High	Medium	Not applicable	Medium	Not applicable	Medium
3	Company owned Cold site	Low	Low	Low	High	Medium	Low
4	Commercial Hot site	High	High	High	Low	High	High

Table 4-10 Cost-capability ratings

Compared with the pre-arranged (quick-ship) option, the pre-established systems acquisition option requires less recovery effort; results in a higher quality of system recovery; and provides more control over the recovery process. The cost of this type of option, however, is generally much higher than the pre-arranged (quick-ship) option.

Compared to the company-owned cold site, the commercial hot site option requires less recovery effort; results in a higher quality of system recovery; offers better safety compliance; and provides better security controls. This is because the hot site is always equipped and ready for use, whereas, a cold site needs additional effort to setup, configure, and test systems and equipment. The safety and security controls are typically provided as part of the services offered by the hot site vendor. The cost of the hot site option, however, is significantly higher than the cold site option.

If the cost is not a primary concern, an organization may select the following options to be included as part of the continuity strategy based on the above comparison:

IT System and Infrastructure Acquisition Option—pre-established
Alternative IT Recovery Facility Option—commercial hot site

4.3 General Recovery Strategy Considerations

The key to a successful business continuity strategy is to select recovery options based on an evaluation which considers their characteristics and capabilities. For instance, a hot site option requires careful consideration of

- the distance between the recovery site and the primary site, to ensure it is less likely to be affected by the same disaster
- the extent of technical support available during recovery
- the response time to have the hot site available once the disaster is declared

This section provides examples of general considerations for evaluating recovery options.

Alternate IT Recovery Facility Considerations:

1. Consider a location that would not be affected by the same disaster
2. Consider the time it would take for the recovery team to arrive at the location.
3. For the most time critical systems, consider the use of commercial hot sites with dedicated mirrored systems capabilities.
4. To reduce the cost, initially use a hot site to recover critical systems then move to a cold site until the original or a new site becomes available.
5. Avoid reciprocal agreements if the system and equipment compatibility is difficult to achieve or maintain.
6. Ensure that the IT recovery facility has adequate power redundancy, fire protection controls, and physical security access controls.
7. Ensure that the IT recovery facility vendor provides adequate technical support.
8. Select an IT recovery facility vendor with a long history of supporting IT recovery facilities.

Alternate Work Area Considerations:

1. Consider a work area which is at a location not expected to be affected by the same disaster.
2. Consider a contract with a work area vendor for fixed or mobile office work areas.
3. Consider "work from home" as an option.
4. Consider the use of existing remote company locations and spaces.
5. Ensure that the alternate work area is equipped with adequate data and voice communications lines and equipment, and amenities such as bathrooms and showers.
6. Ensure both remote and local personnel can access the alternate office work area.
7. Consider the use of hotel conference rooms for the crisis management center.
8. Ensure the alternate work area is equipped with office resources such as fax, copiers, white boards, and stationary.

Off-site Storage Facility Considerations:

1. Consider a storage location which is at a safe distance away from the primary site, where it is unlikely to be affected by the same disaster.
2. Ensure that the hours of operation of the storage vendor meet the storage and retrieval requirements.
3. Ensure that the storage facility can adequately protect the storage media from moisture and temperature damages.
4. Ensure that the storage facility has adequate security and safety controls.
5. Ensure that the storage facility vendor has proper storage media handling procedures.

6. Select a storage vendor with a long history of supporting storage facilities.

IT Systems and Infrastructure Acquisition Considerations:

1. For systems with a Recovery Time Objective (RTO) of less than eight hours, use a pre-established system acquisition strategy where alternate systems are acquired prior to the disaster event.
2. For systems with a Recovery Time Objective (RTO) of less than 72 hours but greater than eight hours, use a pre-arranged (quick-ship) strategy where alternate systems are delivered after a disaster within an agreed time period.
3. For systems with a Recovery Time Objective (RTO) greater than 72 hours, use an acquire-as-needed acquisition strategy where the alternate systems are acquired after the disaster event.
4. Use identical replacement systems where possible.
5. Ensure replacement systems are fully tested for recovery prior to a disaster.
6. Frequently test each system separately, and with other systems.
7. Ensure voice and data network systems and equipment have sufficient capacity for recovery.

Manufacturing and Production Recovery Considerations:

1. For critical equipment with a short Recovery Time Objective (RTO), use a pre-established system acquisition strategy where the replacement equipment is acquired prior to the disaster event.
2. Where possible, replace older model equipment with newer models, which are easier to repair and replace in the event of a disaster.

3. Augment the alternate manufacturing and production facility with measures such as redundant HVAC equipment or backup power generators.

4. Ensure that the alternate manufacturing and production facility complies with safety and environmental regulations.

5. Consider maintaining a backup of critical parts at an off-site facility.

6. Consider stocking a supply of raw material/product inventory at a remote warehouse.

7. Establish reciprocal arrangements with other similar organizations for recovery assistance.

8. Consider establishing an agreement with a vendor to salvage and restore any damaged equipment and resources in the event of a disaster.

4.4 Recovery Contracts and Service Level Agreements

Recovery contracts and Service Level Agreements (SLAs) are a means for ensuring proper implementation of the selected recovery options. Written contracts and agreements must be comprehensive and should account for any conditions that can hinder or prevent successful recovery. As a simple example, consider a hot site as an option for an alternate IT recovery facility for highly time-critical systems. Even though this option satisfies the recovery requirements, the recovery may be hindered if the contract allows the vendor to use untested compatible equipment instead of identical replacement equipment. An effective contract will either restrict the recovery to identical replacement equipment or allow an exception for the use of compatible equipment only if it has been pretested and validated for recovery, prior to a disaster.

Commercial contracts and agreements—for work areas, IT systems and infrastructure, and manufacturing and production recovery areas—should clearly specify the following:

1. Availability of the facility, with the required setup and configurations, within the acceptable time period for recovery.
2. Adequate frequency and time for testing the facility for recovery.
3. Adequate work area for staff.
4. Sufficient recovery time.
5. Access to technical support.
6. Adequate capacity for voice and telecommunication links.
7. Availability of identical replacement equipment.
8. Guaranteed access to a recovery facility through alternate arrangements in the event that the facility is being used by any other organization.
9. Clearly stated roles and responsibilities for both vendor's support personnel and the organization's recovery team.
10. Secure and easy access to the facility.
11. Process for controlling changes to systems, equipment, facilities, and resources.
12. Procedures to renew the contract.

While many of the above concerns also apply to reciprocal agreements, there are certain aspects of reciprocal agreements that are unique. Organizations should ensure that reciprocal agreements can accommodate the following:

1. Sufficient additional capacity to recover the partner systems, equipment, work areas, communication links, etc.
2. Security controls to protect sensitive data and information while allowing the other organization to conduct disaster recovery efforts.

3. The time required to setup the facility as an alternate recovery facility once the disaster is declared by the other organization.

4. Safety conditions stated in the recovery requirements.

5. Environmental safety requirements (such as lead free, dust free, chemical free, etc.)

6. Sufficient testing time required to validate the recovery process.

7. Alternate arrangements in the event that the existing facility or equipment is unavailable.

8. Procedures to notify the other party of changes to facility, systems, and equipment.

The terms and conditions in any of the recovery related contracts and agreements must be carefully reviewed by the organization's legal departments. It is also important to investigate the short- and long-term financial and operational status of potential recovery vendors and organization to support the recovery requirements.

Appendix 4A: Examples of Availability Time Concerns for Recovery Options

As indicated in Section 4.2.3 *Phase C: Availability Time Assessment*, most recovery options require a detailed assessment of various concerns that can adversely impact their availability time. Tables 4-11 to 4-19 show examples of availability time concerns (ATCs) for recovery options mentioned in Section 4.2.2 *Phase B: Recovery Options Identification*. The list below describes each table in terms of its corresponding recovery area and one or more recovery requirements.

- Table 4-11: ATCs for alternate office work areas and crisis management center
  Recovery Area: Work areas
  Recovery Requirements:
    a) Alternate office work areas
    b) Crisis management center

- Table 4-12: ATCs for critical IT systems and infrastructure
  Recovery Area: IT systems and infrastructure
  Recovery Requirements:
    a) Critical IT systems and infrastructure

- Table 4-13: ATCs for alternate IT recovery facilities
  Recovery Area: IT systems and infrastructure
  Recovery Requirements:
    b) Alternate IT recovery facilities

- Table 4-14: ATCs for critical equipment and resources
  Recovery Area: Manufacturing and production,
  Recovery Requirements:
    a) Critical equipment and resources

- Table 4-15: ATCs for critical products
  Recovery Area: Manufacturing and production
  Recovery Requirements:
    b) Critical products

- Table 4-16: ATCs for alternate manufacturing and production facilities
  Recovery area: Manufacturing and production
  Recovery requirements:
    c) Alternate manufacturing and production facilities

- Table 4-17: ATCs for critical data and off-site data storage facilities
  Recovery Area: Critical data and critical/vital records
  Recovery Requirements:
    a) Critical data and off-site data storage facilities

- Table 4-18: ATCs for critical data and off-site data storage facilities
  Recovery Area: Critical data and critical/vital records,
  Recovery Requirements:
    b) Critical/vital records and off-site critical/vital record storage facilities

Recovery Option Category	Recovery Options	Examples of Availability Time Concerns
Commercial	Mobile site	The travel distance, route, and traffic congestions may impact the delivery of the mobile site.
	Hotel meeting rooms	The recovery can be impacted by the time needed to find a suitable hotel with available rooms. This can be a major concern if the disaster occurs at a regional local level.
	Fixed site	The distance and travel time needed by staff to reach the site can impact the recovery time.
Company Owned	Alternate company owned site or branch office	The distance and travel time needed by staff to reach the alternate company site can impact the recovery time.
Employee Owned	Home office	The additional coordination and communication is needed between home offices to maintain centralized control can impact the recovery time.
Operational Readiness	Work area (cold site)	A work area in a cold site can take considerable time to prepare the site to receive, install, and configure equipment.
	Work area (warm site)	A work area in a warm site can take between several hours to a day in preparation time before it becomes ready for use.
	Work Area (hot site)	A work area in a hot site is always equipped and ready for use. It can be available within hours.
Critical Resource Acquisition Method	Pre-established	The resources are acquired and installed prior to the disaster; therefore, this option shortens the recovery time.
	Pre-arranged (quick-ship)	The delivery of the resources is guaranteed within an agreed time period by the suppliers. Additional time needed for setup and configuration may impact recovery time.
	Acquire-as-needed	The required resources are ordered from the supplier after the disaster event. As such, they may not be available and ready for use within the expected time for recovery.

Table 4-11: ATCs for alternate office work areas and crisis management center

Recovery Option Category	Recovery Options	Example of Availability Time Concerns
System Acquisition Method	Pre-established	The systems are acquired and installed prior to a disaster; therefore, this option is suited for services that need to be recovered within hours to a few days.
	Pre-arranged (quick-ship)	The delivery of the systems is guaranteed within an agreed time period by the suppliers. Additional time is needed for setup and configuration of systems. This option can typically support the recovery requirements for services within a time frame of 2 to 7 days.
	Acquire-as-needed	The required systems are ordered from the supplier after a disaster event, and may not be available and ready for use within the expected time for recovery. This option can support the recovery requirements for services that can sustain an outage ranging from days to weeks or longer.

Table 4-12: ATCs for critical IT systems and infrastructure

Recovery Option Category	Recovery Options	Example of Availability Time Concerns
Ownership	Company owned remote site	The distance and travel time needed by staff to reach the dedicated alternate company site can impact the recovery time.
	Mobile site	Untested mobile site configuration may affect the recovery time. The travel distance, route, and traffic congestions may impact the delivery of the mobile site.
	Reciprocal site involving a separate organization	Additional time is required to prepare the site for recovery if the site is being used by the partner organization at the time of the disaster. The distance and location the staff must travel to reach the alternate site can affect the recovery time. Delays can also result from the requirements to comply with the partner organization's policies and operational requirements.
	Commercially available dedicated facility	The distance and travel time needed by staff to reach the dedicated alternate recovery facility can impact the recovery time.
	Commercially available shared facility	Additional time is required to prepare the site for recovery if the site was recently used by another organization for testing or to recover from a disaster. The distance and location the staff must travel to reach the alternate shared site can impact the recovery time.
Operational Readiness	Cold site	Requires significant time to acquire, setup, and install equipment – possibly up to two or three weeks.
	Warm site	It has some of the necessary hardware, software and voice communication equipment pre-installed. Additional time ranging from days to one or two weeks may be required for procuring, installing, and configuring additional equipment.
	Hot site	The hot site is always equipped and ready for use. As such it is typically available within hours.

Table 4-13: ATCs for alternate IT recovery facilities

Recovery Option Category	Recovery Options	Example of Availability Time Concerns
Acquire-as-needed	Acquire equipment	Manufacturing equipment which tends to be expensive and unique in design is generally not stockpiled and can take several months of lead time to acquire.
	Acquire parts	In some cases the supplier may stockpile the parts to support equipment maintenance. The lead to time to acquire parts if they are stockpiled can take several days; otherwise, parts have to be manufactured which may take several months.
Pre-established	Maintain contracted services to salvage and restore	In many cases, the extent of the damage can be minimized by salvaging equipment, thereby reducing the time to recover. In some cases, however, the effects of the disaster event may not allow salvage and restore operations to begin immediately. For instance, a fire may produce additional contaminations such as PCBs that would prevent entry for weeks.
	Maintain a backup of critical parts at an off-site facility	The lead time to retrieve the backup parts depends on the distance between the off-site storage facility and alternate recovery facility, parts packaging, and shipping method.
	Maintain backup of critical equipment at an off-site facility	The lead time to retrieve the backup equipment depends on the distance between off-site storage facility and alternate recovery facility, equipment packaging, and shipping method.

Table 4-14: ATCs for critical equipment and resources

Recovery Option Category	Recovery Options	Example of Availability Time Concerns
Backup Surplus Inventory	Maintain a surplus of raw materials and products needed during recovery time at a remote warehouse.	The lead time to retrieve the backup raw material depends on the distance between the remote warehouse and alternate recovery facility, equipment packaging, and shipping method. The products could be shipped to customers directly from the remote warehouse with no affect on the recovery time.
Production Assistance	Make arrangements with competitors to supply products	The competitor may delay the supply of products in situations where it is at a full capacity at the time of the disaster, or its own customers are waiting for the same product.
	Make reciprocal arrangements with other similar organizations for production assistance	The partner organization may delay the supply of product in situations where it is at a full capacity at the time of disaster, or its own customers are waiting for the same product.

Table 4-15: ATCs for critical products

Recovery Option Category	Recovery Options	Example of Availability Time Concerns
Alternate Recovery Facility	Use company's existing empty facility at another location	The site will need considerable preparation time to install equipment and satisfy unique production or regulatory requirements.
	Acquire a separate commercially available site as needed	Recovery time can be affected by the additional time required to find a suitable commercial site and by the time needed to negotiate the lease. Additional delays are expected due to the preparation time needed to install equipment and satisfy unique production or regulatory requirements.
	Rebuild or repair the damaged site	Recovery time can be impacted by the time needed to assess the damage and recoverability condition, prepare an insurance claim, and assign a contract to rebuild, and to rebuild and satisfy safety and other regulatory requirements.
	Share company's other existing manufacturing facility for production	Recovery time can be impacted by the time needed to re-arrange existing configurations to accommodate operations of the original damaged facility.

Table 4-16: ATCs for alternate manufacturing and production facilities

Recovery Option Category	Recovery Options	Example of Availability Time Concerns
Data Backup Frequency	Continuous	Suitable for RPO of few hours
	Daily	Suitable for RPO = 1 day
	Weekly	Suitable for RPO = 1 week
	Monthly	Suitable for RPO = 1 month
Backup Type	Full	Compared to incremental and differential backups, restoration from a full backup requires the fewest tapes and the shortest recovery time.
	Differential	Compared to incremental backups, restoration requires fewer tapes and shorter recovery time.
	Incremental	Incremental backup types require the most tapes and time to recover.
Backup Method	Remote mirroring	Suitable for continuous availability requirements where RTO = 0; RPO = 0
	Transaction routers	
	Wide Area High Availability Clustering	Suitable for services with RTO < 8 hours and RPO < 30 minutes.
	Storage Area Network (SAN)	
	Storage Virtualization	
	Disk Mirroring	
	Disk Shadowing	
	Application or Utility based data replication	
	Electronic Vaulting	Suitable for services with RTO > 8 hours and RTO < 72 hours; and RPO < 24 hours.
	Remote Journaling	
	Tape backups	Suitable for services with RTO > 72 hours; and RPO > 24 hours.
Off-site Storage Facility	Commercial data storage facility	The distance between the off-site commercial storage facility and alternate recovery facility and the backup media shipping method can impact recovery time.
	Company owned remote data storage facility	Retrieval of backup media can be delayed if company staff must travel to the off-site storage facility to obtain it. The distance between the off-site storage facility and alternate recovery facility, and the shipping method can impact the recovery time.

Table 4-17: ATCs for critical data and off-site data storage facilities

Recovery Option Category	Recovery Options	Example of Availability Time Concerns
Backup Frequency	Daily	Suitable for RPO = 1 day
	Weekly	Suitable for RPO = 1 week
	Monthly	Suitable for RPO = 1 month
	Yearly	Suitable for RPO = 1 year
Storage Media	Microfilm	The time needed to reproduce information to original form, such as paper, can have a potential impact on the recovery time. This depends on the timely availability and efficiency of the reproduction equipment such as microfiche readers, tape readers, etc.
	Microfiche	
	Optical disk	
	Magnetic tapes	
	Disks	
	CD	
Salvage and Restore Method	Pre-arranged contract with a vendor for salvage and restore operations	In many cases, the extent of the damage can be minimized by salvaging critical records, thereby, reducing the time to recover.
	Contract on an as-needed basis for salvage and restore operation	Considerable time is needed to find a suitable contractor and negotiate an agreement to salvage and restore critical records.
Off-site Storage Facility	Commercially operated record storage facility	The distance between commercial off-site storage facility and alternate recovery facility, and the backup record shipping method can impact the recovery time.
	Company owned remote record storage facility	Retrieval of records can be delayed if company staff must travel to the off-site storage facility to obtain them. The distance between the off-site storage facility and alternate recovery facility, and the shipping method can impact recovery time.

Table 4-18: ATCs for critical record and off-site record storage facilities

Chapter 5
Business Continuity Plan Development

5.1 Chapter Overview

The business continuity plan is developed during the fourth stage of the BCP process (see Figure 1-3). The business continuity plan contains predetermined recovery procedures and guidelines which organizations can follow during a crisis to minimize impact on the business. The predetermined procedures and guidelines prevent organizations from making on-the-spot critical decisions in the middle of a crisis.

To a certain extent, Business Continuity Planning (BCP) is similar to the way planning occurs in our personal lives. Consider an example of planning a long distance driving trip with the objective to reach a specific destination within a certain time frame. The travel plan contains phases such as preparation, travel, and stopovers, as well as resources and sequence of activities and tasks involved in each phase, such as obtaining maps, finding directions, driving, eating meals, and resting. A travel plan is also based on a strategy which helps the driver to select various travel options such as the fastest routes (versus the safest routes) or renting a car (versus using ones car). BCP shares the following similarities compared with the travel planning example:

- Planning is designed to achieve an *objective* at a future time.
- Planning deals with the complexity of the problem by dividing the solution into *phases*.
- Planning identifies *resources*, *activities*, and *tasks* needed to complete each phase.
- Planning relies on certain *strategies* for achieving the objective.

The objective of the business continuity plan is to recover critical processes within a certain time frame. The business continuity plan addresses a sequence of events called phases as depicted in Figure 5-1: initial response and notification, problem assessment and escalation, disaster declaration, plan implementation logistics, recovery and resumption, and normalization. Descriptions of these phases specify personnel, resources and activities[1] needed to achieve the objective.

The personnel, resources, and activities, taken together, implement the recovery options selected by the business continuity strategy. The recovery options can consist of, for instance, either a pre-established, pre-arranged (quick-ship), or acquire-as-needed option for acquiring IT and non-IT resources. They could also specify a cold site, warm site, or hot site option for an alternate recovery facility. These recovery options are discussed in Chapter 4 *Business Continuity Strategy Development*.

The next section of this chapter identifies essential elements of the business continuity plan through an example outline. The remainder of the chapter explains the content of each element.

---

[1] The business continuity plan specifies high-level activities, procedures, and tasks which are defined as follows: a high-level activity consists of one or more procedures and a procedure consists of one or more tasks.

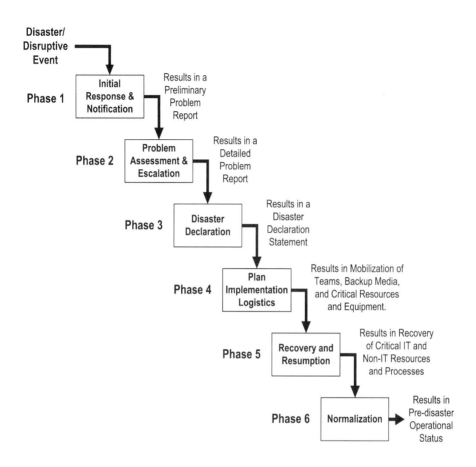

Figure 5-1: Business continuity plan execution phases

5.2 Business Continuity Plan Outline

Business continuity plans vary in structure and content from one organization to the next because of differing business needs. Any business continuity plan is acceptable if it is both comprehensive and feasible:

- Comprehensive—plan takes into account recovery of all critical processes, and consider all recovery phases: initial response and notification, problem assessment and escalation, declaration, logistical preparation, critical applications and resource recovery, and transition to normal operation.

- Feasible—plan is up-to-date, flexible, and is not difficult to implement through the available budget, teams, resources, and facilities.

At a minimum, the business continuity plan needs to address certain essential elements such as those listed in the following outline[2]. Each element within the outline includes a reference (in parentheses) to the section of this chapter that explains the element in detail.

Example Business Continuity Plan Outline:

1. Objective and Scope (*Section 5.3*)
2. Definition of a Disaster (*Section 5.4*)
3. Risk Management Summary (*Section 5.5*)
4. Business Impact Analysis Summary (*Section 5.6*)
5. Business Continuity Strategy Summary (*Section 5.7*)
6. Business Continuity Teams (*Section 5.8*)
7. Contact Information (*Section 5.9*)
8. Activities for BC Plan Execution Phases (*Section 5.10*):
   a. Initial Response and Notification (*Section 5.10.1*)
   b. Problem Assessment and Escalation (*Section 5.10.2*)

---

[2] Additional elements of a business continuity plan such as an introduction, executive summary, title, and names of authors are not addressed in this book.

    c. Disaster declaration (***Section 5.10.3***)

    d. Plan Implementation Logistics (***Section 5.10.4***)

    e. Recovery and Resumption (***Section 5.10.5***)

    f. Normalization (***Section 5.10.6***)

9. Mapping Resources to BC Plan Execution Phases, Activities, Procedures, and Tasks (***Section 5.11***)

10. Assigning Activities, Procedures, and Tasks (***Section 5.12***)

11. BC Plan Change Control (***Section 5.13***)

12. BC Plan Appendices (***Section 5.14***):

    a. Emergency Response Plan

    b. Crisis Communication Plan

    c. External Contacts

    d. Critical Office Work Area Equipment and Resource Information

    e. Critical IT Systems and Infrastructure Information

    f. Critical Manufacturing and Production Equipment and Resource Information

    g. Critical Manufacturing and Production Products

    h. Critical Data and Critical/Vital Records

    i. Alternate IT Recovery Facility Information

    j. Alternate Manufacturing and Production Facility Information

    k. Alternate Office Work Area Information

    l. Crisis Management Center Resource Information

    m. Critical Data and Critical/Vital Record Storage/Retrieval Procedure

    n. Insurance Policy Information

    o. Service Level Agreement Information

    p. BCP Guidelines and Standards Information

    q. Forms

    r. Risk Assessment Report Information

    s. BIA Report Information

    t. Business Continuity Strategy Report Information

    u. Business Continuity Plan Distribution List

    v. Glossary

The sections in the remainder of the this chapter describe these key plan elements in detail. Appendices at the end of this chapter provide additional information related to an emergency response plan, a crisis communication plan, and critical data and records:

- Appendix 5A *Emergency Response Plan Requirements*

- Appendix 5B *Crisis Communication Plan Requirements*

- Appendix 5C *Critical Data and Critical/Vital Records Off-site Storage Requirements*

5.3 Objective and Scope

The objective of the business continuity plan is to reduce consequences of a disruption to an acceptable level through execution of pre-established continuity and recovery procedures. Continuity and recovery of critical processes identified during the BIA are the main focus of the business continuity plan.

The scope of the business continuity plan specifies the operational and technical areas—both inside and outside the organization—that are covered by the plan. Below are some areas typically addressed in the scope:

- Specific company sites and locations;
- Business units;

- Alternate IT recovery facilities, alternate office work areas, alternate manufacturing and production facilities, and crisis management center;
- Off-site storage facilities for data and vital records;
- Business partners and customers;
- Suppliers of critical IT and non-IT equipment and resources;
- Civil authorities (fire, police, and ambulance services).

This section also includes additional scope related information such as:

- The maximum length of time assumed for recovery operations.
- Types of events that can invoke the plan, such as loss of critical services, disk failures, and lack of access to buildings.
- Areas not addressed by the plan. For example, the plan may not address specific remote business locations, or it may cover disruption to data communication services but exclude voice communication services.

5.4 Definition of a Disaster

The purpose of defining a disaster in the business continuity plan is beneficial both during the plan development stage and immediately following a business disruption. A concise disaster definition provides clear focus during plan development. Following a business disruption, a pre-established definition of a disaster helps to determine whether or not the disruption qualifies as a disaster and thus whether to involve the measures in the plan, or address the interruption through other means, such as standard operational procedures, outsourcing the response, or some other means.

The following is an example of a disaster definition: A disaster is an event that disrupts mission-critical business processes and degrades their service levels to a point where the resulting financial and operational impact to an organization becomes unacceptable.

The disaster definition section of the plan also classifies a disaster according to its severity level. The purpose of disaster classification is to help the business continuity teams determine appropriate responses in a timely manner during a crisis situation. Minor, intermediate, and major represent an example disaster classification. This classification is described below.

5.4.1 Minor Level Disaster

This type of disaster occurs more frequently in normal day-to-day operations, compared to an intermediate or a major disaster. The severity level is considered minor because the effects are often isolated to a small subset of critical business processes. The business units that depend on these critical processes can still continue to operate for a certain length of time. The cause of the disruption is often the failure of a single component, system, or service. Example causes of minor level disasters can be failures of manufacturing equipment parts, system disks, and voice network hardware.

5.4.2 Intermediate Level Disaster

An intermediate level disaster occurs less frequently but with greater impact compared to the minor level disaster. This kind of event disrupts normal operations of some but not all critical business units. The operational disruptions result from major failures of multiple systems and equipment. Example causes of the intermediate level disaster include water leakage into the computer room, structural damage to the part of the building housing critical equipment, etc.

5.4.3 Major Level Disaster

The possibility of this type of disaster occurring is very small but the extent of the impact is significant compared to the minor and intermediate level disasters. This event disrupts normal operations of most or all of the critical business processes. The operational disruptions are the result of inaccessibility or failure of most or all of the systems and equipment. Example causes of this type of disaster can include destruction of or inability to access company facilities due to fires, earthquakes, storms, or sabotage.

5.5 Risk Management Summary

This section of the plan summarizes the risks to the organization. Information for this section is extracted from the risk assessment report produced in stage 1 of BCP process (see Section 2.3.4 *Phase IV: Risk Reporting*). The risk management summary should include the following information:

1. A list of threats and risks
2. A list of critical assets exposed to the threats
3. A list of implemented risk controls and residual risks

This section should also include a reference to the risk assessment report for additional information.

5.6 Business Impact Analysis Summary

This section of the plan summarizes the BIA findings related to the critical business processes. The BIA is conducted during the second stage of the

BCP process (see Chapter 2 *Business Impact Analysis*). The summary should list the critical processes and their recovery requirements in terms of the following:

1. Maximum Tolerable Downtime (MTD)
2. Critical IT systems and applications
3. Critical non-IT resources
4. Recovery Time Objectives (RTOs), Recovery Point Objectives (RPOs), Work Recovery Times (WRTs) of critical applications and resources

This section should include a reference to the BIA report for additional information.

5.7 Business Continuity Strategy Summary

During the business continuity strategy development stage, various options were investigated for recovering disrupted data, records, applications, systems, equipment, and facilities. This section summarizes the recovery options selected for the following recovery areas and requirement categories:

- **Recovery Area:** Work areas
  Recovery Requirement Categories:
    a) Alternate office work areas, for staff to perform work
    b) Crisis management center, for crisis management team to conduct recovery efforts

- **Recovery Area:** IT systems and infrastructure
  Recovery Requirement Categories:
    a) Critical IT systems and infrastructure

b) Alternate IT recovery facilities

- **Recovery Area:** Manufacturing and production
  Recovery Requirement Categories:
  a) Critical equipment and resources
  b) Critical products
  c) Alternate manufacturing and production facilities

- **Recovery Area:** Data and critical/vital records
  Recovery Requirement Categories:
  a) Critical data and off-site data storage facilities
  b) Critical records and off-site record storage facilities

This section should include a reference to the business continuity strategy document for accessing additional information.

5.8 Business Continuity Teams

This section of the business continuity plan defines the organization of the business continuity teams, and their roles and responsibilities. The size and the number of teams depend on the scope and complexity of the plan.

Figure 5-2 describes a typical business continuity team structure. In this structure, teams are classified into three layered groups representing crisis management, business resumption, and technical and operational recovery.

Members of a team are chosen based on their knowledge and experience of activities, procedures, and the tasks assigned to the team. Ideally, teams are staffed with the personnel who perform the same or similar tasks under normal conditions. For example, operating system recovery team

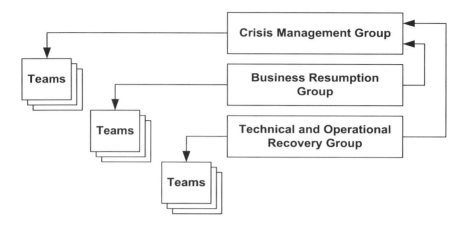

Figure 5-2: Business continuity plan team structure

members should include operating system administrators. If possible, each member is designated as an alternate for another team member in the event he/she is unavailable during the recovery period. Team members are expected to be familiar with the goals and procedures of other teams to facilitate intra-team activities.

This section of the plan should also address the possibility that a disaster can prevent most team members from participating in the recovery effort. To deal with such situations, teams should include members from other geographic areas such as staff from remote company branches, vendor personnel, and contractors.

Each team is led by a team leader who directs overall team operations, acts as the team's representative to management, and liaises with other team leaders. The team leader disseminates information to team members and approves any decisions that are made within the team.

The rest of this section provides a brief description of the teams and their responsibilities.

5.8.1 Crisis Management Group

The Crisis Management Group consists of

1. Crisis Management Team (CMT),
2. Business Continuity Coordinator (BCC),
3. Damage Assessment Team (DAT),
4. Notification Team (NT),
5. Emergency Response Team (ERT),
6. Crisis Communication Team (CCT),
7. Resource Procurement and Logistics Team (RPLT), and
8. Risk Assessment Manager (RAM).

Crisis Management Team (CMT)

The CMT manages and controls the execution of the business continuity plan, emergency response plan, and crisis communication plan. The requirements for an emergency response plan and crisis communication plan are described in Appendix 5A *Emergency Response Plan Requirements* and Appendix 5B *Crisis Communication Plan Requirements*. During the initial and subsequent periods of the crisis, the CMT uses a crisis management center to conduct its operations.

It is essential for this team to have at least one senior manager as the team leader, responsible for its overall guidance. The organization's chief operating officer is an example of a person for this role. The CMT leader has the final decision and authority to invoke the plan. Other members of the team include the business continuity coordinator, and leaders of emergency response, damage assessment, crisis communication, notification, resource procurement and logistics, and risk assessment teams. These members provide information about their teams' activities to the CMT. The CMT can include representatives from IT, human resources, legal, and finance departments, as well as representatives from relevant business units.

Figure 5-3 illustrates the crisis management team in relation to crisis management, business resumption, and technical and operational recovery groups.

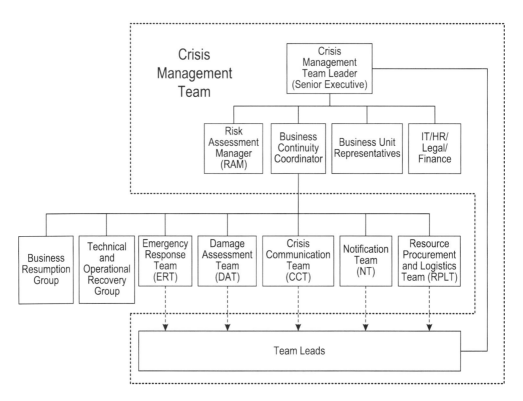

Figure 5-3: Crisis management team

Business Continuity Coordinator (BCC)

The BCC has the overall responsibility for managing the plan execution phases: initial response and notification, problem assessment and escalation, disaster declaration, plan implementation logistics, recovery and resumption, and normalization. The BCC coordinates the activities and provides an important communication link between the CMT and other teams. The BCC is also responsible for the development, testing, and maintenance of the plan.

Damage Assessment Team (DAT)

The DAT is mobilized immediately after the occurrence of a disruption. It is responsible for assessing the extent of the damage based on pre-established guidelines, and for estimating the time to recover.

Notification Team (NT)

The NT is responsible for notifying business continuity teams and personnel needed to execute the plan and its recovery procedures. The notification is performed according to pre-established notification procedures. An example notification method using contact lists is described in Section 5.9 *Contact Information*.

Emergency Response Team (ERT)

The ERT is responsible for protecting life, property, and the environment immediately after a disruption. The ERT facilitates personnel evacuations, internal rescue operations, medical assistance, and incident containment. By coordinating activities with fire, police and ambulance departments, the ERT attempts to stabilize the situation. ERT uses an emergency response plan containing procedures and guidelines for handling emergency situations. Appendix 5A *Emergency Response Plan Requirements* at the end of this chapter details general requirements for an emergency response plan and includes descriptions of emergency response team members and their responsibilities.

Crisis Communication Team (CCT)

The CCT is responsible for providing consistent, timely, and accurate crisis information to staff, management, external business partners, customers, and public. Based on pre-established communication guidelines, specified in the crisis communication plan, the CCT provides information regarding the nature of the disruption, its status, actions that are being taken, and expected recovery time. Guidelines for the crisis communication plan are identified in Appendix 5B *Crisis Communication Plan Requirements*, at the end of this chapter.

Resource Procurement and Logistics Team (RPLT)

RPLT is responsible for ensuring expedient and timely acquisition of resources and equipment needed for recovery. It is also responsible for mobilizing people, resources, equipment, and supplies to the alternate recovery facilities.

Risk Assessment Manager (RAM)

The role of Risk Assessment Manager (RAM) is to assess and control the risks associated with the disruption and the execution of the business continuity plan. The assessment includes risks related to security, insurance, legal obligations, and safety.

5.8.2 Business Resumption Group

The business resumption group consists of the User Management Team (UMT) and a number of Business Unit Teams (BUT).

Figure 5-4 illustrates the business resumption group.

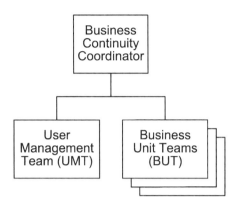

Figure 5-4: Business resumption group

User Management Team (UMT)

The UMT's role is to conduct an overall assessment of the user departments' immediate needs, monitor the recovery progress and status, and coordinate the recovery activities between the business unit teams and the IT technical recovery teams (defined below). The UMT consists of main leads from the business unit teams.

Business Unit Teams (BUT)

A business unit team represents a single business unit. Its membership consists of key users of critical systems and resources. The role of BUT is to assess the current needs of the unit, and assist the IT technical recovery team to recover lost data and resources, re-enter manually kept data, and to validate successful recovery.

5.8.3 Technical and Operational Recovery Group

The technical and operational recovery group is illustrated in Figure 5-5. This group consists of IT and non-IT resource recovery teams as listed below:

1. IT Technical Recovery Teams (ITTRT)
2. Manufacturing and Production Technical Recovery Team
3. Safety and Hazardous Material Handling Team
4. Vital Records Salvage and Restoration Team
5. Data and Critical Record Backup Retrieval Team
6. Administration Support Coordination Team
7. Restoration Team

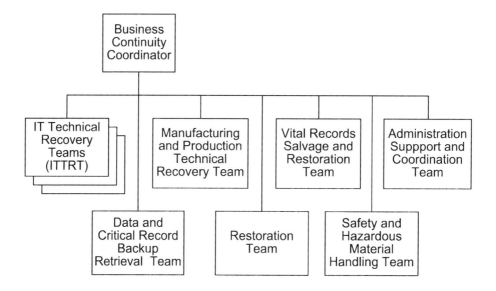

Figure 5-5: Technical and operational recovery group

The teams in the technical and operational recovery group are described in the following sections.

IT Technical Recovery Teams (ITTRT)

IT technical recovery teams consist of a number of different teams, each focused on the recovery of a specific technical area. Example of these teams include

- Operating Systems Platform Team,
- Networking and Telecommunications Team,
- Database Systems Team,
- Applications Team,
- Systems Backup Team,
- Security Control Team, and
- Integration and Testing Team.

Manufacturing and Production Technical Recovery Teams (MPTRT)

These teams are responsible for the salvage and recovery of critical manufacturing and production equipment and resources. Examples of these teams include:

- Equipment Damage Assessment and Salvage Team,
- Equipment Repair and Restoration Team,
- Equipment Testing Team,
- Safety Control Team,
- General Support Team,
- Mechanical Engineers,
- Equipment Technicians, and
- Electricians.

Safety and Hazardous Material Handling Team

This team assists with both the recovery task at the alternate recovery facilities, and the restoration of the damaged site. It is responsible for inspecting unsafe conditions and contaminations, and implementing proper safety controls. Depending on the type of potential hazards involved, this team can include fire safety inspectors, hazardous material specialists, representatives from utility companies (gas, water, electrial), and experts in toxicology, microbiology, etc.

Vital Records Salvage and Restoration Team

The objective of this team is to salvage damaged records by providing immediate and special care to prevent further loss, and to apply procedures that help to restore records to their original conditions. The safety and hazardous material handling team assists this team with the salvage and restoration effort.

Data and Critical Record Backup Retrieval Team

This team is responsible for retrieving from the backup facility copies of operating systems, applications, data, critical records, and manuals and documents needed for recovery. It is also responsible for ensuring security of the backup media. It is important that at least one member of this team is from the organization's record management department or group to assist the team with the retrieval of critical and vital records.

Administration Support Coordination Team

This team's role is to coordinate the recovery process with alternate recovery facilities, off-site storage facilities, and hardware/software vendors. It is responsible for food, accommodations, and travel arrangements, as well as for tracking expenditures.

Restoration Team

Responsibility of the restoration team is to facilitate transition from the alternate recovery facility to the original facility or a new facility.

5.9 Contact Information

Contacting personnel spread across the organization tends to be difficult under normal conditions; in a disaster it can prove to be even more difficult to contact the teams and their members. Therefore, it is critical to maintain accurate and up-to-date contact information within the business continuity plan.

A common approach for maintaining contact information is to use a "call tree" along with a "contact list". A call tree is a hierarchical structure that represents team members and their notification sequence. A team member represented as a node in the call tree list is notified by another member at a higher level node if they are linked together. Each node for a team member in the call tree should reference another member of the team designated as an alternate contact person.

An example call tree for the IT technical recovery teams is depicted in Figure 5-6.

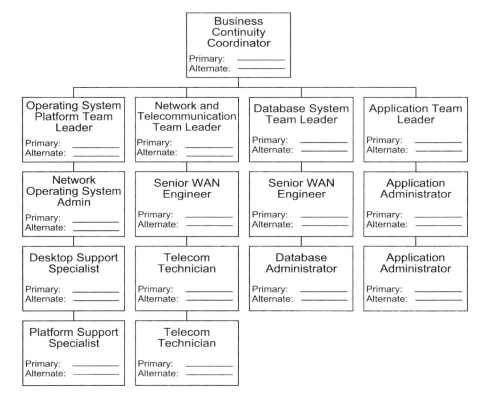

Figure 5-6: Sample call tree for IT technical recovery teams

A contact list contains information on how to contact each member. There may be more than one contact list. For instance, a master list with names of all contacts in alphabetical order, and a list for each business continuity team with each individual on the list having the following information:

- Team name
- Member's name
- Member's role

- Office telephone number
- Cell phone number
- Pager number
- Home number
- Email address
- Alternate team member (used in the event that the primary member is not reachable)
- Expected notifications and communications

The expected notifications and communications entry indicates the correspondence the team member will receive when the business continuity plan is executed. The notification team, for instance, uses this information to notify and deliver communications to appropriate teams. The communication may include the preliminary problem report, detailed problem report, or disaster declaration statement. The type of communication that members will receive depends on their role as defined in the member's role field.

Critical contact information regarding suppliers, service providers, and customers is attached to the business continuity plan as an appendix (see the *External Contacts* appendix in Section 5.14 *BC Plan Appendices*).

5.10 Activities for BC Plan Execution Phases

This part of the document describes various phases for executing the plan. Figure 5-1 shows typical business continuity plan execution phases:

- **Phase 1: Initial Response and Notification**
  A preliminary problem report is prepared as an immediate response to a disruption. Appropriate teams are notified based on the type and extent of the damage.

- **Phase 2: Problem Assessment and Escalation**
  A detailed problem report is prepared after a thorough inspection of the disrupted site. Appropriate teams are notified based on the findings in the detailed problem assessment report.

- **Phase 3: Disaster Declaration**
  The detailed problem report is reviewed and a decision is made on whether or not to declare a disaster. A disaster declaration statement is prepared in this phase. The remaining phases are executed once a disaster is declared.

- **Phase 4: Plan Implementation Logistics**
  Logistical procedures are executed to prepare the recovery environment and mobilize the required teams and resources for the recovery and resumption, and normalization phases.

- **Phase 5: Recovery and Resumption**
  Critical IT and non-IT resources are recovered and critical process work is resumed at the following facilities: alternate IT recovery facility, alternate office work area, alternate manufacturing and production facility, and crisis management center.

- **Phase 6: Normalization**
  The environment and operations are normalized to pre-disaster conditions by transitioning from an alternate recovery facility to either the restored original site or to another facility such as a cold site.

These six phases are presented in Figure 5-7 on a time line starting with a disaster event.

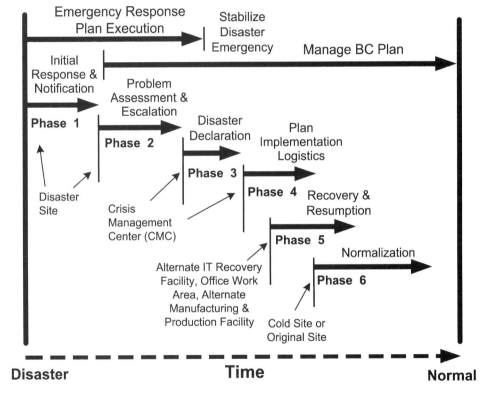

Figure 5-7: Business continuity plan execution phases

A disruptive event may trigger execution of both the emergency response plan and the business continuity plan. The emergency response plan focuses on the safety of employees and protection of the organization's assets. It contains procedures to stabilize an emergency through coordination with the civil authorities such as fire, police, and ambulance departments. Appendix 5A of this chapter contains general requirements for an emergency response plan.

The execution of the business continuity plan begins with Phase 1 *Initial Response and Notification* and results in the preliminary problem report. Phase 2 *Problem Assessment and Escalation* follows Phase 1 and results in a detailed problem report. If the findings of these two phases indicate a serious business impact, the crisis management group is mobilized to manage the execution of the business continuity plan. The main focus of phase 1 and 2 is the disrupted site.

Phase 3 *Disaster Declaration* is executed by the crisis management team. Phase 4 *Plan Implementation Logistics* begins once the disaster is declared. Phases 3 and 4 are normally executed at the crisis management center.

Phase 5 *Recovery and Resumption* occurs at the alternate recovery facilities. Phase 5 can begin during the same time period as Phase 4. For instance, recovery at the alternate office work area may begin as soon as the required logistics are completed; even though, logistics for other alternate recovery facilities have not been completed.

Phase 6 *Normalization* typically focuses on the restoration of the damaged site or a cold site.

The remainder of this section describes the six business continuity plan execution phases in more detail.

5.10.1 Phase 1: Initial Response and Notification

The initial response and notification phase begins immediately after the disruption. In this phase, the business continuity coordinator is alerted; the business continuity plan is activated; the damage and extent of the impact are assessed at a high level; and notification is sent to the crisis management team, damage assessment team, and fire and safety authorities if needed.

The business continuity plan specifies activities for appropriate teams to follow. These are sample high-level activities[3] for this phase:

1. Receive initial alert regarding the disruption from on-site personnel, senior management, emergency response team or safety authorities.
2. Alert fire and safety authorities (if required) unless they have already been notified.
3. Access business continuity plan related documents.
4. If the disruptive event occurs during non-business hours, travel to the facility.
5. Determine if the facility is accessible.
6. Notify and mobilize damage assessment team.
7. Conduct a preliminary assessment of the damage.
8. Conduct a preliminary assessment of the cause of the damage.
9. Conduct a high-level evaluation of the extent of the damage impact.
10. Prepare a preliminary problem report.
11. Notify the notification team.
12. Notify the crisis management team.

The preliminary problem report prepared during activity 10 above provides an overview of the cause and extent of the damage. Appropriate teams are notified through activities 11 and 12 according to the information contained in the preliminary problem report.

---

[3] The business continuity plan specifies high-level activities, procedures, and tasks which are defined as follows: a high-level activity consists of one or more procedures and a procedure consists of one or more tasks.

5.10.2 Phase 2: Problem Assessment and Escalation

The objective of this phase is two-fold: first, determine the extent of the problem based on the preliminary problem report produced in the preceding phase; second, decide whether or not to escalate the problem to the next phase.

These are sample high-level activities for this phase:

1. Receive the preliminary problem report.
2. Review the preliminary problem report for the extent and impact of the damage.
3. Inspect the disrupted site for detailed assessment of disaster impact.
4. Assess health and safety related risks.
5. Assess the building, structural damage, the interruption to manufacturing processes, damaged equipment, etc.
6. Estimate the financial loss.
7. Determine the severity level of the disaster based on the pre-established disaster definition—minor, intermediate, or major (see Section 5.4 *Definition of a Disaster*).
8. If there is no impact to critical processes at the current time, continue to monitor the situation; otherwise, proceed to the next phase of the plan execution.
9. Prepare a detailed problem report.
10. Notify business resumption group teams, and technical and operational recovery group teams via the notification team.

The detailed problem report prepared in activity 8 above, provides detailed information regarding the following:

1. Disaster level;

2. Estimated financial loss;
3. Source of the damage such as fire, flood, and earthquake;
4. Extent and magnitude of the damage such as
   a. building structures affected by the disaster (floors, buildings, neighborhoods);
   b. business units affected by the disaster;
   c. types and number of IT systems, infrastructure, etc.;
   d. number of critical processes disrupted.
5. Physical condition of the original facility;
6. Safety status of the original facility;
7. Presence of hazardous contaminants;
8. Risk of further damage; and
9. Estimated length of the recovery period.

5.10.3 Phase 3: Disaster Declaration

The decision to declare a disaster in this phase is based on the review of the detailed problem report produced by the preceding problem assessment and escalation phase. A suitable recovery approach is selected; a disaster declaration statement is prepared and used as a guideline for the remaining plan execution phases; and appropriate personnel are notified.

Below are sample high-level activities for the this phase:

1. Review the disaster level, risks, and impacts described in the detailed problem report.
2. Review the available recovery options described in the business continuity strategy section.
3. Decide on the best recovery options for the current situation. Two simple examples of recovery options are to recover at the original site or at alternate recovery facilities, or to involve pre-arranged

(quick-ship) or acquire-as-needed arrangements for recovering systems and equipment.

4. Prepare a disaster declaration statement containing the following information:
   a. Occurrence of the disaster
   b. Date and time of the disaster
   c. Selected disaster severity level (minor, intermediate, or major) and descriptions of the possible severity levels.
   d. Selected recovery options
   e. Recovery location information
   f. Estimated time of the recovery
   g. Name of the disaster declaration authority (names of individuals responsible for issuing disaster declaration statement)
   h. Contacts for clarification and additional information
5. Issue disaster declaration statement via the notification team.
6. Notify crisis communication team.

5.10.4 Phase 4: Plan Implementation Logistics

This phase focuses on the logistical tasks of preparing the recovery environment and mobilizing the business continuity teams and resources for the recovery and resumption, and normalization phases. The information from the previous phases (such as the disaster declaration statement and detailed problem report) guide the activities for this phase. For instance, the Resource Procurement and Logistics Team (RPLT) examines the disaster declaration statement and orders the recovery resources according to the selected recovery options.

The following is an example of a list of high-level activities for preparing alternate recovery facilities:

1. Order computer hardware and software.
2. Order voice and data communication equipment.
3. Order faxes, printers, and copiers.
4. Order magnetic tapes and hard disks.
5. Order forms used to track manual procedures.
6. Order electronic calculators and stationery.
7. Ship key documents including business continuity plan to the alternate recovery facility.
8. Prepare for receiving ordered equipment at the recovery facility.
9. Prepare for receiving tapes and critical records at the recovery facility from the off-site storage facility.
10. Prepare the alternate IT recovery facility, alternate office work area, alternate manufacturing and production facility, and crisis management center to accommodate teams.

Team preparation activities ensure that each member of the team has access to the information, resources, and facilities he/she needs to travel to the alternate recovery facility and carry out the assigned tasks. Below is an example list of the activities for preparing teams:

1. Identify who is available for recovery operations.
2. Identify who will be traveling where and for how long.
3. Identify who will be working at the original site if it is still accessible.
4. Identify the resources required such as laptops, maps, copies of the business continuity plan document, and equipment inventory lists.
5. Make the necessary travel arrangements.
6. Provide security clearance for the recovery team to access the alternate recovery facilities.
7. Provide the resources needed.
8. Provide the travel documents.

9. Provide information regarding the point-of-contact at the alternate recovery facilities.

10. Provide information about the technical support available at the alternate recovery facilities.

11. Provide alternate recovery facility contract information including the expected recovery environment and configuration.

12. Provide information on what is being shipped to the alternate recovery facilities.

5.10.5 Phase 5: Recovery and Resumption

The recovery and resumption phase deals with the planned activities at the these facilities:

1. Original damaged facility
2. Alternate IT recovery facility
3. Alternate office work area
4. Alternate manufacturing and production facility
5. Crisis management center

The following sections describe typical activities performed at each of the above facilities.

Original Damaged Facility Activities

The recovery activities at this site are carried out by the technical and operational recovery group. The technical and operational recovery group is responsible for salvaging critical IT and non-IT resources, and vital records. The damaged site activities can be divided into four phases: preparation, inspection and assessment, salvage and restoration, and transportation.

1. Preparation

   a. Ensure all required teams have arrived at the damaged site.
   b. Ensure teams have the list of critical resources at the damaged site.
   c. Ensure team members have proper safety equipment.
   d. Review detailed problem report.
   e. Review safety procedures and guidelines.

2. Inspection and Assessment

   a. Inspect building and utilities (water, gas, electrical, etc.).
   b. Inspect the resources and vital records for any hazardous contamination such as chemicals, molds, PCB, and asbestos.
   c. Inspect the resources and vital records for the type of damage such as water, fire, dust, and ice.
   d. Inspect the resources and vital records for the extent of damage.
   e. Assess the potential for further damage or deteriorations.
   f. Determine the salvage and restoration recovery options.
   g. Determine the length of time available to apply salvage procedures to prevent further deterioration.
   h. Document the inspection and assessment findings.

3. Salvage and Restoration

   a. Acquire special salvage and restoration equipment/resources as needed.
   b. Remove hazardous contaminants if required.
   c. Execute procedures to avoid further deteriorations such as by controlling the humidity and temperature to prevent growth of molds on water damaged resources and vital records.
   d. If necessary, relocate salvaged resources and vital records to an area better suited for restoration work.
   e. Apply appropriate restoration procedures.
   f. Document the salvage and restoration results.

4. Transportation

a. Determine the location to transport the salvaged and restored resources and vital records, such as an alternate office work area, alternate IT recovery facility, alternate manufacturing and production facility, etc.
b. Prepare guidelines for safe and secure handling of the salvaged and restored resources and vital records.
c. Arrange for transportation.
d. Transport salvaged and restored resources and vital records according to the secure handling guidelines.

Alternate IT Recovery Facility Activities

The activities at the alternate recovery facility can be divided into three phases: preparation, staging critical IT systems and infrastructure, and critical IT applications restoration.

1. Preparation

a. Ensure all required teams and their members have arrived at the recovery facility.
b. Ensure everyone on the team is aware of the recovery time requirements such as MTDs, RTOs, RPOs, and WRTs.
c. Ensure team members have the inventory lists and recovery procedures.
d. Review the equipment at the alternate recovery facility and ensure that it is consistent with recovery requirements, for instance, in terms of equipment quantity, type, and size configurations.
e. Review handling procedures for shipped equipment.
f. Receive network related shipped equipment.
g. Receive off-site backup media.
h. Inspect the integrity of the backup media.

i. Inspect the shipped equipment once it arrives and ensure it is consistent with the list of shipped inventory referenced in the business continuity plan.

2. Staging Critical IT Systems and Network Infrastructure

a. Review floor layouts for IT systems and LAN infrastructure, and ensure that they are properly located.
b. Review network diagram and ensure proper location and connectivity of LAN infrastructure and equipment such as servers, bridges, gateways, routers, etc.
c. Ensure all critical IT systems are connected to the network.
d. Review the network and system addressing and configuration information.
e. Run procedures to configure modems and controllers.
f. Restore LAN data from backup media to network servers.
g. Restore security systems including firewalls.
h. Redirect voice and data network to the alternate IT recovery facility.
i. Provide network and system interfaces to alternate office work areas and alternate manufacturing and production facilities.
j. Test and verify network connectivity.

3. Critical IT Application Restoration

a. Review recovery priorities for critical IT systems and applications.
b. Review the next highest priority critical IT system and application restoration procedure.
c. Ensure passwords are available.
d. Restore operating systems from backup media.
e. Configure operating systems.
f. Verify network connectivity.
g. Restore applications from backup media.
h. Verify application functionality.

  i. Restore data from backup media.

  j. Verify integrity of the data and its currency.

  k. Ensure application is accessible from alternate office work areas and alternate manufacturing and production facilities.

  l. Hand over applications to users.

Alternate Office Work Area Activities

Alternate office work area activities can be divided into three phases: preparation, staging office work area office equipment and computer infrastructure, and process restoration.

1. Preparation

  a. Ensure all required teams and their members have arrived at the alternate office work area.

  b. Ensure everyone on the team is aware of the recovery time requirements, such as MTDs, RTOs, RPOs, and WRTs.

  c. Ensure team members have the alternate office work area inventory lists.

  d. Review the equipment at the alternate office work area and ensure that it is consistent with recovery requirements, for instance, in terms of equipment quantity, type, and size configurations.

  e. Review handling procedures for shipped critical resources.

  f. Receive the network related shipped equipment.

  g. Receive the backup media.

  h. Inspect the shipped equipment once it arrives and ensure it is consistent with the list of shipped office work area inventory referenced in the business continuity plan.

2. Staging Alternate Office Work Area Office Equipment and Computer Infrastructure

a. Review the floor layout for office furniture.
b. Setup office furniture and assign desks to team members.
c. Review the floor layout for setup of computer infrastructure.
d. Review network diagram.
e. Setup and install office work area LAN.
f. Setup and install workstations, printers, etc.
g. Ensure workstations and printers are connected to the network.
h. Setup copiers and faxes.
i. Setup telephones.
j. Provide office stationeries and supplies.
k. Provide documents and manuals retrieved from off-site storage.
l. Redirect voice and data network to alternate office work area.
m. Ensure network connectivity between office work area and alternate recovery facility LANs.
n. Setup help desk at the alternate office work area.

3. Process Restoration

a. Restore user workstations.
b. Ensure workstation user identifications and passwords are known to users.
c. Restore workstation data using backup media.
d. Receive critical records from off-site storage.
e. Receive and process requests/transactions manually until the systems are recovered at the alternate IT recovery facility.
f. Take over the recovered systems and verify the data and application integrity.
g. Recover work backlog by entering the manually collected data into the system.
h. Begin using the recovered systems for processing any new request/transactions.

Alternate Manufacturing and Production Facility Activities

Alternate manufacturing and production facility activities can be divided into three phases: preparation, staging the manufacturing and production facility, and test equipment and products.

1. Preparation

a. Ensure all required teams and their members have arrived at the alternate manufacturing and production facility.

b. Ensure everyone on the team is aware of the recovery time requirements such as MTDs, RTOs, RPOs, and WRTs.

c. Ensure the manufacturing and production facility complies with safety requirements and standards.

d. Ensure the facility's environmental conditions, such as dust and humidity levels, are conducive to maintaining the required quality standards for equipment and products.

e. Inspect the adequacy of the storage area for hazardous materials.

f. Inspect the facility for safety controls.

g. Ensure sufficient electrical power and wiring is in place for operation of machines and equipment.

h. Ensure team members have the alternate manufacturing and production facility inventory lists.

i. Review the equipment at the site and ensure that it is consistent with recovery requirements; for instance in terms of equipment quantity, type, and size configurations.

j. Review handling procedures for shipped equipment and parts.

k. Receive any shipped critical equipment and parts.

l. Receive any shipped surplus products and inventories.

m. Inspect the shipped equipment once it arrives and ensure it is consistent with the list of shipped manufacturing and production facility inventory lists.

2. Staging Alternate Manufacturing and Production Facility

a. Review floor layout for manufacturing equipment and machinery, and products setup.
b. Setup manufacturing equipment and machinery.
c. Setup copiers and faxes.
d. Setup telephones.
e. Provide equipment operation documents and manuals retrieved from the backup storage.
f. Redirect voice network to manufacturing and production facility.
g. Setup computer workstations and LAN equipment.
h. Setup network connectivity between manufacturing and production facility, and alternate IT recovery facility LANs.

3. Test Equipment and Products

a. Test equipment and machinery.
b. Test products.
c. Test voice communication network.
d. Test connectivity between manufacturing and production facility and alternate IT recovery facility.
f. Ensure workstation user identifications and passwords are known to users.
g. Restore workstation data using backup media.

Crisis Management Center (CMC) Activities

The first task at the CMC is to prepare the facility for crisis management activities. The following are example preparation tasks:

a. Ensure all required teams and their members have arrived at the crisis management center.

b. Review the equipment at the facility and ensure that it is consistent with the work area requirements for CMC, for instance in terms of equipment quantity, type, and size configurations.

c. Inspect the shipped equipment once it arrives and ensure it is consistent with the list of the CMC inventory.

d. Ensure the existence of uninterruptable power supplies, water, and communication lines.

e. Review the floor layout for office areas, meeting rooms, etc.

f. Setup office furniture and assign desks to team members.

g. Provide a laptop with overhead projection for presenting business continuity plan and related information.

h. Review floor layouts for setup of computer infrastructure.

i. Setup and install workstations, printers, etc.

j. Ensure workstations and printers are connected.

k. Setup copiers and faxes.

l. Setup telephones.

m. Provide office stationery and supplies.

n. Provide documents and manuals retrieved from off-site storage.

Once the preparations are complete, the crisis management team can begin the planned activities. Their activities can be grouped into a number of different areas such as alternate recovery facilities, crisis communication, human resources, finance, insurance, and legal. Examples of activities in these areas are given below.

Alternate Recovery Facilities

1. Oversee recovery, resumption, and normalization phases.
2. Review the recovery progress with respect to the MTDs.
3. Assess risks.
4. Resolve problems, issues, and risks.
5. Decide if additional capacity and/or recovery time is needed at the alternate recovery facilities.

Crisis Communication

1. Activate the crisis communication plan, if it is not already activated through the disaster declaration phase.
2. Oversee communication messages and ensure they are delivered.

Human Resources

1. Keep track of staff not available for work due to injuries, vacations, deaths, etc.
2. Provide support (medical, financial, and legal) to injured staff and their families.
3. Provide support to families of staff who may have lost their lives.
4. Prepare a head count of staff available for normal operations and recovery operations.
5. Hire temporary staff if needed during the disaster recovery period.
6. Keep track of time spent by contractors and staff on regular and overtime work during the recovery period.
7. Disburse salaries to staff and payments to contractors.
8. Ensure staff is rotated on shifts to allow for adequate rest periods.

Finance

1. Review financial status of the organization and ensure availability of sufficient cash flow to pay creditors, suppliers, and staff.
2. Ensure bills and invoices are issued and outstanding payments are received on time from customers and business partners.
3. Keep track of the spending during the recovery period.
4. Estimate the cost of repairing facilities and resuming normal operations.
5. Provide financial condition assessments to senior management.

Insurance

1. Review the property and casualty insurance documents.
2. Notify insurance company regarding the disaster.
3. Conduct an internal insurance claim assessment for disaster loss.
4. Gather documents and records required for insurance claims.
5. Submit loss estimates and required documents and records to the insurance company.
6. Review the discrepancies between the internal assessment and the insurance company's assessment.
7. Review the insurance document for any clauses indicating the maximum time allowed for appealing the loss discrepancies.
8. Notify the senior management regarding insurance claim status and issues.

Legal

1. Notify company lawyers.
2. Review legal and legislative due diligence requirements.
3. Review legal issues related to injuries,death, and property damage.
4. Review contract documents for legal implications.

5.10.6 Phase 6: Normalization

In this phase arrangements are made to return either to the original site or to go to another site such as a cold site. The objective is to return the environment and operations to pre-disaster conditions. There are four stages of activities associated with this phase, namely, site determination, site repair, preparation, and transition. With the exception of the transition stage, all other stages can occur in parallel with recovery and resumption phase activities. The transition stage begins once the recovery and resumption phase is complete. Example activities for the original facility determination, site repair, and preparation stages are listed below.

Original Facility Determination

1. Review the inspection and assessment findings prepared by the technical and operational recovery group during the recovery and resumption phase.
2. Determine the feasibility of returning to the original site.
3. Explore the option to move to another site such as a cold site.
4. Consult with senior management to determine a transition site.

Repairs

1. Approve repairs to the damaged site.
2. Hire contractors to repair the damaged site.
3. Supervise repairs.
4. Obtain required government permits such as building safety and occupation permits.
5. Review the inventory of damaged equipment for types, model, quantity, and configuration; and place orders to replace equipment.
6. Receive and inspect ordered equipment.
7. Install power and LAN cables.
8. Install phone lines.
9. Install office furniture.
10. Install and test workstations, printers, telephones, copiers, etc.
11. Supply stationery.

Preparation

1. Review network diagram and ensure proper location and connectivity of LAN infrastructure equipment such as servers, bridges, gateways, routers, etc.

2. Install systems.
3. Ensure all critical IT systems are connected to the network.
4. Review the network and system addressing and configuration information.
5. Run procedures to configure modems and controllers.
6. Restore LAN data from backup media to network servers.
7. Restore security systems including firewalls.

Transition

1. Determine the time frame for transition.
2. Notify team of transition schedule and task assignments.
3. Freeze production environment at the alternate recovery facility.
4. Prepare full data backups of the alternate recovery facility environment.
5. Prepare shipments of vital records and documents to original or new site.
6. Transfer team, data backups, and vital records to original or new site.
7. Restore IT systems, applications, and data at original or new site.
8. Verify environment such as network, application, data, etc.
9. Compare and verify the application and data with that at the alternate recovery facility.
10. Redirect voice and data network to original or new site.
11. Provide new passwords and user identifications to users.
12. Distribute vital records.
13. Resume normal operation.
14. Initiate normal backup procedures.
15. Setup technical support line.
16. Clean up alternate recovery facilities in accordance with the contract and security procedures. Destroy secret or confidential data and applications residing on the IT systems at the alternate recovery facilities. Remove and discard confidential documents remaining at the alternate recovery facilities.

5.11 Mapping Resources to BC Plan Execution Phases, Activities, Procedures, and Tasks

The purpose of this section is to associate each resource with the business continuity plan execution phases, high-level activities[4], procedures, and tasks in which the resource is utilized. There are two steps needed to create this mapping: first, determine procedures and tasks required for each high-level activity in the business continuity plan execution phases; and second, map each resource to the business continuity plan phases, activities, procedures, and tasks.

Determining Procedures and Tasks

Each high-level activity in a business continuity plan execution phase may have one or more lower level procedures. In turn, each procedure may be have one more lower level tasks. For example, the "Send Notification" activity for the notification team can be accomplished through the procedures and tasks indicated below.

1. Procedure: review disaster declaration statement.
2. Task: review the call tree(s), and notify appropriate personnel.
3. Task: review the contact list(s), and notify appropriate personnel.

This section must include the procedures and tasks needed to accomplish each high-level activity specified in the business continuity plan execution phases.

---

[4] The business continuity plan specifies high-level activities, procedures, and tasks which are defined as follows: a high-level activity consists of one or more procedures and a procedure consists of one or more tasks.

Mapping Resources to BC Plan Execution Phases, Activities, Procedures, and Tasks

Table 5-1 shows an example mapping of an EDI server and application resource to the business continuity plan execution phases, activities, procedures, and tasks.

Resource	BC Plan Execution Phase	Activity Name/ID	Procedure Name/ID	Task Name/ID
EDI server and application	Phase 4 Plan Implementation Logistics	Order IT systems and applications (PL: 1)	Order EDI server hardware application (PL: 1, a)	Obtain EDI server and application server (PL: 1, a, 4) Place order (PL: 1, a, 5) Update list of shipped IT systems and applications (PL: 1, a, 6)
	Phase 5 Recovery and Resumption	Setup, install and configure IT systems and applications (ITTRT: 2)	Setup, install, configure EDI server hardware (ITTRT: 2, b)	Setup EDI server hardware components (ITTRT: 2, b, 1) Install EDI server operating system (ITTRT: 2, b, 2) Configure EDI server operating system (ITTRT: 2, b, 3)
			Install and configure EDI application (ITTRT: 2, c)	Install EDI application (ITTRT: 2, c, 1) Configure EDI application (ITTRT: 2, c, 2)

Table 5-1: Example resource mapping to activities, procedures, and tasks

5.12 Assigning Activities, Procedures, and Tasks

The business continuity plan specifies the organization of the business continuity teams, and their roles and responsibilities (see Section 5.8 *Business Continuity Teams*). The business continuity plan execution phases specify high-level activities needed to complete the phase (see Section 5.10 *Activities for BC Plan Execution Phases*).

The purpose of this section is as follows:

1. Assign high-level activities to business continuity teams.
2. Assign procedures and tasks (identified in the preceding section) to team members.
3. Provide any additional useful information for managing and controlling activities, such as a time line for high-level activities.

Each business continuity plan execution phase specifies high-level activities needed to complete the phase. The business continuity teams and their team members are assigned predefined procedures and tasks that are used to implement the high-level activities.

The information in this section of the plan can be represented through a set of tables such as tables 5-2, 5-3, and 5-4. These tables show example activities, procedures, and tasks for the notification team.

Table 5-2 indicates the team's identification number, name, reference to its predefined roles and responsibilities, and the team leader. Table 5-3 shows each team member's identification number, name, reference to his/her roles and responsibilities, and the business unit to which he/she belongs. In this case, additional tables are needed to represent team roles and responsibilities, and team member roles and responsibilities.

Team Identification Number	Team Name	Reference to Team's Roles and Responsibilities	Team Leader
NT	Notification Team	Reference to NT in team roles and responsibilities table	Smith, G.

Table 5-2: Business continuity team responsibilities

Team Members Identification Number (ID)	Member's Name	Reference to Member's Roles and Responsibilities	Team Member's Functional Unit
6807	Smith, G	Reference to entry in table of team member roles and responsibilities	HR

Table 5-3: Business continuity team member responsibilities

BC Plan Execution Phase	Activity Name/ID	Procedure Name/ID	Task Name/ID	Activity/ Procedure/ Task ID Dependency	Team Assigned	Team Member(s) Assigned/ ID	Reference to Related Documents
Phase 3 disaster declaration phase	Send notification (NT: 1)	Review disaster declaration statement (NT: 1, a)	Determine appropriate call list(s) and notify personnel (NT: 1, a, 1) Determine appropriate contact list(s) and notify personnel (NT: 1, a, 2)	Crisis management team: disaster declaration statement activity (CMT: 5)	Notification team	Smith, G (ID 6807)	Reference to call trees and contact lists

Table 5-4: BC plan execution phase activity assignments

Table 5-4 lists business continuity plan phases, and high-level activities. For each high-level activity, Table 5-4 lists its corresponding procedures and tasks; procedure and task dependencies; team assigned to the activity; team member assigned to the activity; and references to related documents to assist with recovery efforts. In this example, the notification team has a reference to the call trees and contact lists.

The procedures and tasks corresponding to a high-level activity must be sufficiently detailed and comprehensive. An example of the procedures and tasks for the business continuity coordinator is given below:

- Receive initial notification of the disruption.
- Manage and lead business continuity plan execution phases.
- Coordinate activities between crisis management team and other teams.
- Dispatch damage assessment team to the disaster site for assessment.
- Notify risk assessment manager.
- Receive and evaluate preliminary and detailed problem report.
- Inform crisis management team members to evaluate the situation.
- Review risk assessment report.
- Inform and assemble notification team.
- Ensure that teams are properly assembled and executing their responsibilities.
- Oversee funds and expenses.
- Arrange security access to alternate recovery facilities for business continuity teams.
- Monitor recovery activities.
- Document status, progress, problems, and issues.

Table 5-5 lists each high-level activity and its begin and end times. This information is useful for managing and controlling activities. For instance, the begin and end times can be mapped to a time line that visually represents each activity.

BC Plan Execution Phase	Activity Name/ID	Begin Time (relative to the time of disaster)	End Time (relative to the time of disaster)
Phase 3 disaster declaration phase	Prepare disaster declaration statement (CMT: 5)	55 minutes	70 minutes
	Send notification (NT: 1)	70 minutes	80 minutes

Table 5-5: BC plan execution phase activity begin and end times

5.13 BC Plan Change Control

Organizations experience frequent changes in terms of people, processes, and technology. The business continuity plan needs to be synchronized with these changes to ensure its readiness and the accuracy of its recovery information. The changes to the business continuity plan document must be controlled through change control procedures in order to maintain the plan's integrity and validity. This section contains procedures for updating and revising the business continuity plan. These procedures are part of Step 3 *Process BC Plan Change Requests*, in the business continuity plan change management process described in Chapter 7 *Business Continuity Plan Maintenance*.

A formal change request form is useful for requesting revisions and updates to the plan. A blank change request form should also be included in the plan (see the *Forms* appendix in Section 5.14 *BC Plan Appendices*). In addition to using the change request form, this section of the plan must include a record of all changes to the business continuity plan.

An example of a high-level change control procedure is described below. This procedure assumes that a change request form is submitted for processing as part of the change control management process and that there is a change manager with the responsibility to coordinate the processing of the change request with the business continuity teams.

1. Review the change request.
2. Determine the nature of the changes required (e.g. people, process, or resource change).
3. Determine the sections or parts of the plan affected by the change.
4. Identify the personnel responsible for the affected areas of the plan who then either create a draft document containing revisions and changes to their respective areas of the plan, or reject the change request related to their part of the plan and document the reasons.
5. Review all draft documents for any dependancies, conflicts, and inconsistencies; and revise the draft documents if necessary.
6. Finalize the draft documents and obtain signatures from authorized personnel.
7. Update the business continuity plan document according to the changes and revisions specified in the approved documents, and apply version control.
8. Record the changes in this section of the plan.
9. Distribute the business continuity plan to the individuals on the business continuity plan distribution list (see "Business Continuity Plan Distribution List" in Section 5.14 *BC Plan Appendices*).

5.14 BC Plan Appendices

Business continuity plan appendices provide additional details and document references that supplement the information in one or more areas of the plan. The following are examples of business continuity plan appendices:

a. **Emergency Response Plan**
   This appendix contains the emergency response plan (see Appendix 5A *Emergency Response Plan Requirements*, for information regarding emergency response plans and a sample plan outline).

b. **Crisis Communication Plan**
   This appendix contains the crisis communication plan (see Appendix 5B *Crisis Communication Plan Requirements*, for a general crisis communication plan outline).

c. **External Contacts**
   This appendix contains contact information for critical suppliers, service providers, and customers (see Section 5.9 *Contact Information*, for details regarding business continuity team call tree and contact list).

d. **Critical Office Work Area Equipment and Resource Information**
   This appendix contains a list of office work area equipment and resources at the original site that support critical business processes. For each item, the list should describe its manufacturer, type, model number, and quantity. Examples of information in this appendix include furniture, workstations, fax machines, printers, telephones, etc.

e. **Critical IT Systems and Infrastructure Information**

This appendix contains a list of IT systems and infrastructure at the original site that support critical business processes. Example information in this appendix includes critical IT systems and applications; LAN, WAN, and voice communication hardware and components such as bridges, routers, switches, firewalls, PBXs, gateways, and servers; and network diagrams. The manufacturer, type, model number, and quantity of the item should be included.

f. **Critical Manufacturing and Production Equipment and Resource Information**

This appendix contains a list of manufacturing and production equipment, and resources at the original site that support critical business processes. Example information in this appendix includes floor layouts, manufacturing equipment, machinery, parts, etc. For each item, the list should describe its manufacturer, type, model number, and quantity.

g. **Critical Manufacturing and Production Products**

This appendix contains a list of manufacturing and production products at the original site that support critical business processes. Example information in this appendix includes list of products, components, raw materials, etc. For each item, the list should describe its manufacturer, type, model number, and quantity.

h. **Critical Data and Records**

This appendix contains a list of critical data and records stored at the off-site storage facility that support critical business functions (see Appendix 5C *Critical Data and Critical/Vital Records Off-site Storage Requirements* for more information on storing data and records in off-site storage).

i. **Alternate IT Recovery Facility Information**

    This appendix contains a list of IT systems and infrastructure at
    the alternate IT recovery facility that support critical business
    processes. Example information in this appendix includes critical IT
    systems and applications; LAN, WAN, and voice communication
    hardware and components such as bridges, routers, switches,
    firewalls, PBXs, gateways, and servers); and network diagrams.
    For each item, the list should describe its manufacturer, type, model
    number, and quantity.

j. **Alternate Manufacturing and Production Facility Information**

    This appendix contains a list of manufacturing and production
    facility equipment, resources, and products such as floor lay-
    outs, network diagrams, manufacturing and production equip-
    ment, machinery, and parts. For each item, the list should describe
    its manufacturer, type, model number, and quantity.

k. **Alternate Office Work Area Information**

    This appendix contains a list of office work area equipment and
    resources at the alternate recovery facility. For each item, the list
    should describe its manufacturer, type, model number, and quantity.
    Examples of information in this appendix include furniture, worksta-
    tions, fax machines, printers, telephones, etc.

l. **Critical Crisis Management Center Equipment and Resource
    Information**

    This appendix contains a list of equipment and resources to
    support the activities of the crisis management team at the crisis
    management center. For each item, the list should describe its type,
    model number, and quantity.

m. **Off-site Data and Critical/Vital Record Storage/Retrieval
    Procedure**

    This appendix contains the procedure for retrieving data and critical/vital records from the off-site storage facility (see Appendix 5C *Critical Data and Critical/Vital Record Off-site Storage Requirements*, for general steps regarding this procedure.

n. **Insurance Policy Information**

This appendix contains summaries and references to property and casualty insurance policies. The information in this appendix should enable the organization to substantiate and recoup losses in a timely manner. Examples of information included in this appendix are adjuster and insurer contact information; insurance coverage details for the damaged property, casualty, and business interruption insurance; claim tasks and procedures; and references to claim forms.

o. **Service Level Agreement Information**

This appendix contains summaries and references to internal and external service level agreements.

p. **BCP Guidelines and Standard Information**

This appendix contains summaries and references to internal and external business continuity planning guidelines and standards.

q. **Forms**

This appendix contains forms to support the business continuity plan. Examples include forms for equipment ordering, insurance claims, business continuity plan change requests, preliminary damage report, detailed problem report, and disaster declaration report.

r. **Reference to Risk Assessment Report**

This appendix contains a reference to the risk assessment report.

s. **Reference to BIA Report**

   This appendix contains a reference to the BIA report.

t. **Reference to Business Continuity Strategy Report**

   This appendix contains a reference to the business continuity strategy report.

u. **Business Continuity Plan Distribution List**

   This appendix contains a list of people to receive copies of the plan, as part of the plan's change control procedures. This list should be carefully defined to prevent distribution to unauthorized individuals and avoid compromising the sensitive and confidential plan information.

v. **Glossary**

   This appendix contains a glossary of common business continuity terms and definitions.

Appendix 5A: Emergency Response Plan Requirements

An emergency response plan contains predetermined guidelines and procedures used to carry out a managed, coordinated, and effective response to an emergency immediately after a crisis. An emergency is any disruptive or harmful event that endangers people, environment, or an organization's property and assets. Examples of disruptive events can include fires, floods, storms, hazardous material spills, riots, and accidents. The emergency can be small, as in a fire contained by employees using fire fighting equipment, or large, as in a disaster resulting from an earthquake or a tornado.

The objective of the emergency response plan is to protect life, environment, and assets, and to bring the crisis under control. The actual response can be carried out by both the internal business organization (employees) and external authorities (fire, police, ambulance, and/or public works departments).

Both emergency response plans and business continuity plans deal with crises: emergency response plans focus on life and safety issues, whereas business continuity plans focus on continuing mission-critical business functions.

5A.1 Emergency Response Team (ERT)

An emergency response plan requires an Emergency Response Team (ERT) to oversee its development, maintenance, and execution. An example ERT may include the following personnel:

- **Emergency Response Team Leader**
  The emergency response team leader is responsible for coordi-

nating all emergency response activities. These include plan activation, evacuation, incident logging and assessment, and notification of business continuity coordinator and civil authorities. The team leader also activates the safety and hazardous material handling team if required. This role is assigned to a person who has experience or training in emergency response activities and is familiar with the organization's staff, facilities, resources, and operational environment.

- **Evacuation Leaders**
  Evacuation leaders are responsible for evacuating personnel to a safe area, keeping track of personnel, and relaying important life and safety related information to the emergency response team leader and civil authorities. An evacuation leader may be assigned to each floor.

- **Medical Staff**
  These are on-site medical staff such as nurses and doctors that can provide immediate emergency medical (first-aid) assistance.

- **Rescue Staff**
  Rescue staff are personnel specially trained in emergency rescue operations.

5A.2 Emergency Response Plan Activation

The emergency response team leader is responsible for activating the emergency response plan by notifying the civil authorities (fire and police departments and ambulance services) and employees, and initiating an evacuation of the affected area. The emergency response team leader also notifies the business continuity coordinator who may then initiate the business continuity plan. Both the emergency response plan and business continuity plan can be executed in parallel.

5A.3 Emergency Response Plan Considerations

An emergency response plan requires careful pre-emergency provisioning and preparations. Prior to developing an emergency response plan, the following high-level elements should be considered:

1. Emergency control functions
   a. Coordination between the emergency response team leader and crisis management team
   b. Incident command system interface and protocols
   c. Provisioning of the crisis management center

2. Communications during emergencies
   a. Primary and alternate emergency communication methods
   b. Emergency incident alerting and escalation methods
   c. Communicating with emergency response team
   d. Communicating with an employees' family members
   e. Communicating with civil authorities

3. Protection of employees, public, assets, and environment
   a. Alerting systems and methods
   b. Evacuation requirements
   c. Shelter provisions
   d. First aid provisions
   e. Equipment and building shutdown requirements
   f. Building protection systems
   g. Hazardous material handling, containment, and clean up

4. Awareness and training

5. Emergency scenarios

5A.4 Emergency Response Plan Outline

The structure and content of emergency response plans can vary from one organization to the next. The intent of this section is to highlight elements that are part of typical emergency response plans through the following example plan outline:

1. Policy, objectives and assumptions
2. Authority and scope
    a. Building/site
    b. Employees
3. Visitors and on-site personnel
4. Emergency response plan maintenance
5. Emergency response team functional description and responsibilities
6. Reference to business continuity plan
7. Reference to crisis communication plan
8. Employee responsibilities
9. General emergency handling procedure and plan activation
    c. Notification of emergency response team
    d. Notification of civil authorities
    e. Notification and evacuation of personnel
10. Evacuation procedures
    a. Alarms, signals, evacuation leaders
    b. Escape routes
    c. Designated assembling areas
    d. Personnel accounting
11. Shelter-in-place procedures
    a. Alarms, signals, evacuation leaders
    b. Designated safe areas
    c. Provisions for shelter areas
12. Search and rescue procedures
13. Building and equipment shutdown procedures

14. Organization-specific emergency response procedures
    a. Fires
    b. Earthquakes
    c. Hazardous material spill control procedures
15. Post-emergency response procedures
16. Appendices
    a. Emergency response contact lists
        i) External civil authorities
            (1) Fire
            (2) Police
            (3) Ambulance
        ii) Emergency response team (primary and alternates)
            (1) Emergency response team leader
            (2) Evacuation leaders
            (3) Medical staff
            (4) Rescue staff
    b. Maps
        i) Escape routes
            (1) Primary route
            (2) Secondary route
        ii) Floor plans
            (1) fire extinguishers
            (2) gas and water lines
            (3) electric panels
    c. Emergency supplies and equipment
        i) First aid supplies
        ii) Hazardous material safety equipment
        iii) Hazardous material clean up equipment
        iv) Fire suppressant equipment

Appendix 5B: Crisis Communication Plan Requirements

A crisis communication plan guides the crisis management team in providing timely, consistent, and accurate information to company personnel, business partners, and the public. The following is an example outline for a crisis communication plan:

1. Communication objectives
2. Authorized communication coordinator
3. Conditions for invoking the plan
4. Plan assumptions
5. List of contacts for issuing updates
6. Message Content
   a. General information:
      i) Notification and clarification of disruptive event
      ii) Impact of the event
      iii) Current status and conditions
      iv) Time of next update
   b. Specific requests or directions for
      i) Employees
      ii) Business partners
      iii) Customers
      iv) Public
   c. Contact details for additional information
7. Means of communication
   a. Media
   b. Telephone (landline, satellite, etc.)
   c. Emails
8. Frequency of communication
9. Crisis communication approval and authorization process.
10. Plan update log

Appendix 5C: Critical Data and Critical/Vital Record Off-site Storage Requirements

Both critical data and critical records are vital to the recovery of business processes. Critical data can include critical IT applications and components needed to support those applications, such as operating systems, databases, and data. Critical records are any documents, drawings, and photographs that are essential for supporting critical business processes. A critical record is considered as vital if it is either irreplaceable or very difficult and expensive to reproduce.

Critical IT applications and critical records were identified during the BIA, Stage 2 of the BCP process. The off-site data and records backup options were selected during the business continuity strategy development stage. The business continuity plan contains information needed to transfer and retrieve backups to and from the off-site storage facility, and to track all backup media and their contents.

This section lists some of the key information needed for tracking and storing critical data and critical records at an off-site storage facility.

5C.1 Critical Data Backup Information

1. Business Unit
   Name of business unit that creates, updates, and destroys the backup data.

2. Backup Owner
   Name and contact information of the individual or department who own this data.

3. Dependent Critical Processes
   Critical processes that depend on data.

4. Recovery Sequence/Priority
   Recovery priority of this data during the retrieval and recovery procedures.

5. Data Category
   Category of the data such as application, operating system, database.

6. Backup Data Name
   Name of the system, application, and database as known within the organization.

7. Storage Format
   Format of the data on the media such as binary or ASCII.

8. Backup Storage Vendor
   Name and contact of the off-site storage vendor.

9. Backup Storage Location
   Address of the off-site storage location.

10. Backup Storage Media
    Storage media that contain the data, such as microfilm, microfiche, optical disk, magnetic tape, disk, or CD.

11. Data Size
    The size of the backup data.

12. Information Confidentiality Level
    Privacy level of the information contained in the backup media, such
    as open, restricted, or top secret.

13. Transportation Information
    Name and contact information of transportation company, shipping
    procedures, and shipping forms.

14. Backup Frequency
    Frequency of backup of data to the off-site storage facility such
    as daily, weekly, monthly, and yearly.

15. Type of Backup
    Type of backup, such as full, incremental, or differential.

16. Backup Storage and Retrieval System
    Commercial software used to store and retrieve data to backup
    media.

17. Media Storage Life
    The length of time the media are reliably used for storage before
    they begin to deteriorate.

18. Backup Record Identification
    Mechanism for uniquely identifying the record such as bar-
    codes and labels.

19. Backup Location and Access
    Exact location where the data is stored such as building and room
    number, shelf number, and drawer number.

20. Safe Data Handling and Preservation Practice
    Recommendation for properly handling and preserving of backup

media in order to prevent damage to the media and loss of the stored information. An example recommendation is as follows: media must be transported and stored in a dust free container at certain temperature and humidity levels to prevent the harmful effects of impurities, heat, and condensation.

5C.2 Critical Record Backup Information

1. Business Unit
   Name of the business unit that creates, updates, and destroys this critical record.

2. Record Owner
   Name and contact information of the individual who owns this record.

3. Dependent Critical Processes
   Critical processes that depend on the use of the record.

4. Recovery Sequence/Priority
   Recovery priority of this record during the retrieval and recovery procedures.

5. Record Information Type
   Type of information contained in the record, such as accounts payable, lease, insurance, operational policy, and equipment inventory.

6. Record Category
   Category of the critical record, such as business form, business document, and legal document.

7. Information Confidentiality Level
   Privacy level of the information contained in the backup media,
   such as open, restricted, or top secret.

8. Off-site Storage Vendor
   Name and contact of the off-site storage vendor.

9. Off-site Storage Location
   Address of the off-site storage location.

10. Type of off-site Storage Media
    Type of storage media that contains the critical record, such as
    microfilm, microfiche, optical disk, magnetic tape, disk, or CD.

11. Record Volume
    The volume of the record in storage in terms of number of
    document pages, file size, etc.

12. Transportation Information
    Name and contact information of the transportation company.

13. Backup Frequency
    Frequency of the backup of the record to the storage facility
    such as daily, weekly, monthly, and yearly.

14. Record Retention Period
    A period of record retention specified as the date of creation to the
    date of final destruction.

15. Backup Storage and Retrieval System and Equipment
    Devices used to store and retrieve the record. For instance, micro-
    photography and microfiche readers are two devices needed to
    store and retrieve documents stored on microfiche.

16. Media Storage Life
The length of time the media are considered reliable for storing critical records before they begin to deteriorate.

17. Record Identification
Mechanism for uniquely identifying the record, such as the bar-code.

18. Record location and Access
Exact location where the record is stored, such as building and room number, shelf number, and drawer number.

19. Record Reproduction Method
Method of reproducing the stored record in specific format and form required during the recovery process. Document format may include, for instance, paper, electronic database, etc.; document form may specify part of the document, complete document, or document summary.

20. Safe Record Handling and Preservation Practice
Recommendation for properly handling and preserving record storage media in order to prevent damage to the media and loss of the stored information.

5C.3 Data and Critical/Vital Record Storage/Retrieval Procedure

Example Storage Procedure

1. Obtain approval for storage from owner of the data or critical/vital records.
2. Obtain the storage vendor's forms to be filled out.

3. Review the safe handling procedure.
4. Review the information confidentiality level and limit access accordingly.
5. Ensure that media storage life is still valid.
6. Verify accuracy of backup frequency and type of backup.
7. Create a record's bar code for tracking and storage.
8. Update the backup inventory.
9. Package the backup media according to the safe handling procedure.
10. Update the backup log for the current backup media.
11. Contact the backup vendor using the contact information.
12. Contact the media transportation company using the transportation information.
13. Transport the media according to the safe handling procedure.

Example Retrieval Procedure

1. Obtain approval for retrieval from owner of the data or critical/ vital records.
2. Obtain the storage vendor's forms to be filled out.
3. Contact the backup vendor using the contact information.
4. Contact the media transportation company using the transportation information.
5. Transport the media according to the safe handling procedure.
6. Update the backup inventory.
7. Review the safe handling procedure.
8. Review the information confidentiality level and limit access accordingly.
9. Verify type of backup and frequency.

Chapter 6
Business Continuity Plan Testing

6.0 Chapter Overview

The business continuity plan is tested in the fifth stage of the BCP process (see Figure 1-3), following the business continuity plan development stage described in the preceding chapter. The value of testing the business continuity plan cannot be overstated. A business continuity plan must not be considered acceptable until it has been completely validated.

The purpose of the testing stage is to validate the business continuity strategy, assumptions, activities, procedures, and guidelines specified in the business continuity plan against likely interruption scenarios; and to identify any gaps and weaknesses within the plan. Certainly, it is highly desirable to find the gaps and weaknesses during a test rather than during a real crisis.

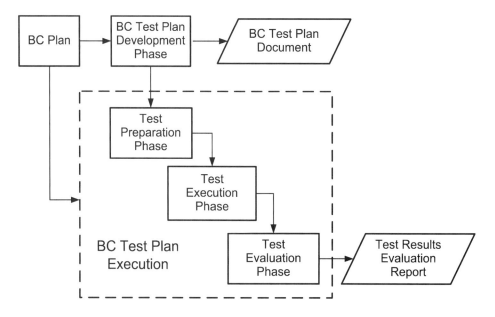

Figure 6-1: Business continuity plan testing phases

The business continuity plan testing stage consists of four phases, as depicted in Figure 6-1:

1. BC test plan development phase
2. Test preparation phase
3. Test execution phase
4. Test evaluation phase

The business continuity plan document provides input to all four of these phases.

The BC test plan development phase results in a BC test plan document containing information needed to conduct the remaining phases and to enable evaluation of the test results (See Section 6.4 *A Framework for Business Continuity Test Plan Development* for detailed steps to develop the BC test plan).

The test preparation phase begins once the BC test plan document is developed. The activities in this phase include meeting with off-site storage vendors and alternate recovery facility providers. The business continuity test teams[1] (BC test teams) visits the alternate recovery facilities in order to become familiar with the facility and its systems, equipment, and resources.

The actual test is conducted during the test execution phase. The BC test plan specifies such details as the date and time of the test and the test method to use. Depending on the scope of the test, this phase covers testing of various parts of the business continuity plan's activities and procedures, and the recoverability of critical systems, equipment, and resources.

The test evaluation phase begins after the test execution phase. This phase evaluates the results of the test execution phase to determine how well test objectives were achieved. The outcome of this phase is a test evaluation report which measures the test successes and failures, and identifies strengths and weaknesses in both the business continuity plan and the test execution. The findings from this phase can help to improve the business continuity plan and future BC test plans, increase the effectiveness of the business continuity teams, and minimize future test expenses.

This chapter is divided into two parts. The first part of this chapter (Sections 6.1 to 6.3) describes the objectives of the business continuity plan testing stage; benefits of business continuity plan testing; and introduces various test methods. The second part of this chapter (Sections 6.4 and 6.5) discuss merits of the business continuity test plan and a structured framework for developing the BC test plan.

---

[1] The teams defined in the business continuity plan form the basis for selecting the business continuity test teams. The structure and size of the business continuity test teams, however, can vary from the teams defined in the business continuity plan depending on test's objectives, scope, and constraints.

6.1 Objective of BC Plan Testing Stage

The testing stage of the BCP process has two main objectives. The first
objective is to determine if the business continuity plan is adequate for
recovering the business within an acceptable time frame. The second
objective is to identify any weaknesses and gaps that may exist in the
business continuity plan. To accomplish these objectives, the testing stage
may involve several tests, each focusing on certain aspects of the overall
test objectives. These tests, for instance, may verify the following:

- Correct and timely execution of the notification procedure and
  accuracy of the information in the call trees and contact lists
- Ability to execute operational tasks to recover systems on an
  alternate platform from backup media
- Completeness of the resource inventory at off-site storage facilities
- Timely arrival of a complete set of backup media
- Integrity of the backup data and ability to restore backups
- Responsiveness of alternate recovery facility providers
- Ability of vendors to deliver hardware within an acceptable
  time frame

6.2 BC Plan Testing Benefits

There are several benefits of testing the business continuity plan:

- Testing validates the functionality of the plan
- Testing identifies weaknesses in the plan
- Testing verifies the currency of the plan
- Testing trains the BC test teams

6.2.1 Validation of BC Plan Functionality

One of the main benefits of testing is that it can validate the functionality of the business continuity plan. The functionality of the business continuity plan is validated if the test objectives were achieved, for example:

1. Successful completion of all procedures and activities in the plan within acceptable time frames
2. Successful recovery of critical processes and resources within the acceptable time frames

6.2.2 Identification of BC Plan's Weaknesses

Testing can reveal gaps and weaknesses in the business continuity plan's activities, procedures, and recovery options. Testing can also identify omissions, such as missing names of crucial team members, critical resources that were never backed-up, missing documents, etc. Finally, testing can expose logistical weaknesses such as delays in the arrival of team members and resources to the alternate recovery facility.

Often, certain details are overlooked during the development of the plan. For instance, licensed software that depends on a Central Processing Unit's (CPU) serial number will not work unless the software is also licensed for the recovery platform CPU's serial numbers. Testing can help to identify these errors so they can be corrected before an interruption.

Execution of the business continuity plan is a team effort. The BC test teams are normally divided into smaller groups responsible for specific activities, procedures, and tasks. Effective team communication is essential for successful recovery. Testing can uncover weak communication points within and across business continuity groups and teams.

6.2.3 Verification of BC Plan's Currency

Organizations can experience many changes related to people, processes, and technology. The test findings can verify if the information in the BC plan is current and consistent with such changes. The following are examples of changes and corresponding test findings which indicate that the information in the BC plan is not current:

1. A team member is not reachable because he/she has moved and the contact information in the call trees or contact lists has not been updated.
2. The vendor for acquiring resources or systems is not reachable. The vendor has merged with a larger company and its telephone numbers have changed.
3. A new service pack was added to an operating system at the production level but certain applications failed during testing due to the lack of the service pack at the recovery site.

6.2.4 Personnel Training

The value of training is obvious for those organizations that have conducted regular testing. The initial test is the most challenging because the BC test teams are often unfamiliar with the information contained in the business continuity plan and the alternate recovery facility. Regular testing improves morale and confidence, and reduces time required to execute procedures and tasks. Testing trains team members to:

- Follow their assigned procedures and checklists, such as system configurations, data recovery from backup media, Local Area Network (LAN) installation, etc.
- Deal with unexpected situations and events, such as undocumented assumptions within the business continuity plan, delays in the arrival of documents, backup tapes, etc.

- Become familiar with alternate recovery facilities, vendor's teams and their culture.

6.3 Test Methods

The following are the main methods for testing the business continuity plan: checklist test, walkthrough test, simulation test, parallel test, full-interruption test, announced test, and unannounced test. As explained in the sections below, these methods vary in terms of costs, effort, and interruptions to normal operations.

6.3.1 Checklist Test

A checklist test is the most basic type of test, and it is generally conducted prior to other more complex types of tests. In it, staff review the business continuity plan, and check the availability and adequacy of information and resources required for executing the plan. The required resources are typically located at the alternate recovery facilities and off-site storage. Some examples of items on the checklist include

1. system and application documents,
2. current telephone numbers on the call trees and contact lists,
3. vital records,
4. backup media,
5. forms,
6. work-around procedures, and
7. application installation manuals.

6.3.2 Walkthrough Test

Walkthrough testing, often called *tabletop testing*, is an inexpensive testing method. It is typically performed prior to conducting a simulation test. In this test, BC test teams meet to verbally describe what activities, procedures, and tasks they will follow. This test allows test team members to become familiar with the business continuity plan, recovery resources, and other team members.

During test preparation meetings, team members are provided with a document describing their assigned procedures and responsibilities. They are also given the test objectives and a scenario for the test. During the walkthrough test, team members walk through their assigned procedures in the presence of the entire team to validate the correctness and effectiveness of the overall plan. During the walkthrough teams and team members assist each other to improve their performance and the plan's procedures.

6.3.3 Simulation Test

In this test, a business disruption is simulated through a disaster scenario. It provides an opportunity for the BC test teams to practice execution of the business continuity plan and to validate one or more parts of the plan. Simulation testing has these characteristics:

1. It can combine both a simulation of plan's activities (which produces simulated results) and actual execution of the plan's activities.
2. It may require testing at the alternate recovery facility.
3. It may require some business units to cease their normal operations.

A simulation test minimizes the cost of testing and interruption to normal operations as a result of the following:

1. Simulating some plan activities instead of actual execution

2. Limiting the number of team members that must travel to the alternate recovery facility

3. Limiting the test scope to certain parts of the plan

The scope of the simulation test may cover one or more activities and procedures of the business continuity plan. These activities and procedures may include the following:

1. Notification procedures
2. Temporary work-around procedures
3. IT system and application installation procedures
4. Recovery of backed-up data
5. Recovery of vital records
6. Recovery of data and voice communications equipment and services

Simulation test results can reveal valuable information about the performance of BC test teams, and any weaknesses and gaps in the tested parts of the business continuity plan.

6.3.4 Parallel Test

A parallel test at the alternate recovery facility runs concurrently with the production environment at the original facility. The production environment continues to function as normal. The systems at the alternate recovery facility are recovered using the last full backup of data. During the time that systems are being recovered at the alternate recovery facility, any transactions at the production environment are recorded manually. These manual transactions are then applied to the systems at the alternate recovery facility. At the end of the test the state of environments at both the alternate recovery facility and original facility are compared. The test is successful if the two environments are identical with respect to the data processed. The parallel test is performed with careful planning, and only after other more simpler types of tests have been successfully completed.

6.3.5 Full-interruption Test

A full-interruption test activates all components of the business continuity plan and assumes all critical business processes are disrupted. The full-interruption test involves all BC test teams, alternate recovery facilities, off-site storage facilities, service providers, and vendors. Unlike the simulation test, this test is larger in scope and involves actual operations and activities specified in the plan. In this test, the BC test teams perform actual operations and activities specified in the business continuity plan compared with the simulation test, which may involve simulated operations and activities.

This type of test is costly and can interrupt normal operations, therefore careful test planning and scheduling is needed to minimize cost and inter-ruptions. Communication and coordination with internal and external business entities are included in this type of test and peak workload peri-ods for critical business processes are avoided.

This test method is recommended once the BC test teams have gained sufficient practice and confidence by thoroughly testing the business conti-nuity plan using other simpler methods such as the simulation test.

6.3.6 Announced Test vs. Unannounced Test

An ideal program for business continuity plan testing combines both an-nounced and unannounced tests methods. In an announced test, the timing and schedule of the test is communicated to the business continuity teams well in advance of the start date. In contrast to an announced test, the timing and schedule of an unannounced test is kept secret from the business continuity teams until the start of the test.

In an announced test members of the business continuity teams have the opportunity to prepare for the test and minimize potential interruptions to their normal day-to-day activities. An announced test, however, fails to test the constant readiness and the ability of the business continuity teams to react in short notice—such a test of the business continuity teams is important because disasters usually occur without warning. An alternative is to use unannounced tests for testing the constant readiness of the teams and their ability to react to the surprise announcement of the test.

An organization should conduct a series of announced tests before attempting unannounced tests. Unannounced tests can begin once the business continuity teams have gained appropriate training and confidence in announced tests. As a precaution, limit the scope of the initial unannounced test, for instance, to a single business unit. For subsequent unannounced tests, gradually expand their scope as the teams gain confidence in this type of test.

6.4 BC Test Plan Document

Initiating a test without proper preparations and planning not only increases the risk of failure but can also damage the reputation and spirit of the BC test teams. Participants in the test may regard the test as a waste of time and effort, and may not cooperate in the next test. In addition, it may become difficult to obtain management's approval for the next test because of the costs and effort incurred in previous unsuccessful tests.

A business continuity test plan is a document that provides guidance for preparing and executing the test. It conveys critical information to the BC test teams, such as:

- What parts of the business continuity plan are to be tested?
- When and where will the test occur?
- What resources are involved?

- Who will conduct the test?
- What activities occur before, during, and after the test?
- How will the test be evaluated?
- Who will observe the test?

The business continuity test plan must be reviewed by the teams to ensure the following:

- The test plan is accurate, up-to-date, and does not contain any gaps
- The test plan is cost-effective
- The test plan is feasible
- The test plan contains realistic and practical test objectives and scenarios
- Team members understand what is expected of them before, during, and after the test

The next section describes a framework for developing the BC test plan.

6.5 A Framework for BC Test Plan Development

Developing a business continuity test plan is a complex process that involves careful analysis of test resources, environment, and activities. A structured approach is recommended to manage the complexity of developing the test plan. Figure 6-2 presents a structured BC test plan development framework which consists of eight steps:

Step 1: Review Previous BC Test Plans and Results
Step 2: Identify Test Objectives and Scope
Step 3: Assess Test Constraints

Step 4: Develop Test Strategy

Step 5: Specify Test Logistics

Step 6: Specify Test Schedule

Step 7: Identify Test Risks

Step 8: Integrate BC Test Plan Components

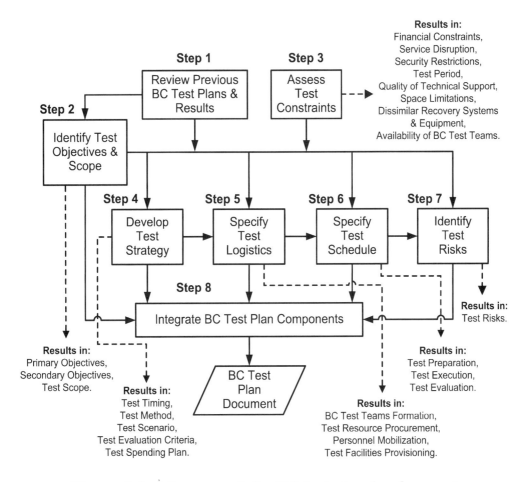

Figure 6-2: A framework for BC test plan development

Step 1 leverages the information and experience gained from previous test plans and results by extracting relevant information to help with the development of the current test plan in steps 2, 4, 5, 6, and 7. Step 2 identifies test objectives and scope. Step 3 assesses constraints that can impact the test strategy, logistics, schedule, and its execution. The results from steps 1, 2, and 3 provide input to steps 4, 5, 6, and 7. A test strategy is developed in step 4 based on the information from steps 1, 2, and 3. Logistical aspects of the test are specified in Step 5 using the information from steps 1 through 4. A test schedule is specified in Step 6 using the information from steps 1 through 5. Step 7 identifies and assesses potential testing risks. Finally, the results of the preceding steps are integrated to produce the BC test plan document in Step 8. Each of these steps are explained in detail in the following sections.

6.5.1 Step 1: Review Previous BC Test Plans and Results

Previous BC test plans and their results are a source of valuable information for developing the current test plan. The information, for example, is useful in identifying the current test objectives. Previous test plans and their results are reviewed to determine the following:

1. Components and areas of the business continuity plan that have not been tested
2. Components and areas of the business continuity plan that worked well
3. Components and areas of previous BC test plans that did not work well

Components and areas that have not been tested or that did not work well become part of the current test plan's test scope.

The information contained in the previous BC test plan and the results of its execution are useful input to develop the current test plan, particularly if both plans contain similar test objectives and scope. The information contained in the previous BC test plan can be extracted to develop the test strategy, logistics, and schedule for the current BC test plan. Challenges and obstacles encountered during execution of the previous BC test plan can help to identify test risks in the current BC test plan.

6.5.2 Step 2: Identify Test Objectives and Scope

The second step in the framework identifies test objectives and test scope. This information becomes the basis for developing the rest of the test plan.

Test Objectives

Test objectives define the criteria for a successful test. Therefore, it is essential to define the test objectives in concise and measurable terms.

Because the time and budget available for testing is often limited, it is helpful to divide the test objectives into primary and secondary objectives. Primary objectives focus on areas of the business continuity plan that must be achieved in order to consider the test successful. Secondary objectives include areas of the business continuity plan that are desirable to test, yet the failure to do so does not render the test unsuccessful. Secondary objectives are assigned a lower priority for testing purposes compared to the primary objectives, and therefore, they are only attempted if time and resources are available.

The following are samples of primary objectives:

1. Determine whether or not the business continuity plan is current
2. Determine the adequacy of the available resources (e.g. vital records, personnel, or supplies)

3. Determine the effectiveness of the backup procedures
4. Determine the ability of the BC test teams to execute the business continuity plan
5. Restore network and operating systems at the alternate recovery facility
6. Restore critical applications identified in the business continuity plan

These are samples of secondary objectives (assuming they are not covered by the primary objectives):

1. Recover a specific distributed application
2. Reroute communication to the recovery facility
3. Test transition to either the original or the cold site once the recovery at the alternate site is complete

Test Scope

The test scope, which identifies the overall depth and breadth of the test, can range from testing specific parts of the business continuity plan to testing the entire business continuity plan. The test scope describes

1. phases, activities, and procedures of the business continuity plan to be tested;
2. business units and BC test teams required to conduct the test; and
3. business partners, vendors, and suppliers assisting with the test.

The test scope should also explicitly identify any key areas of the business continuity plan that will not be tested.

6.5.3 Step 3: Assess Test Constraints

Test constraints are factors that limit or restrict the options available for conducting the test. A clear understanding of the test constraints and their potential effects on a test is essential for developing the test strategy, logistics, and schedule. Some examples of possible test constraints are listed below:

- **Financial Constraints**
  A limited test budget, due to financial constraints, can affect the test in a number of ways. For example, it can restrict the number of team members that can travel to the alternate recovery facility, length of time the alternate recovery facility is available for testing, and choice of recovery systems and equipment available for testing.

- **Service Disruption**
  The test should minimize any service disruptions to business operations. The BC test plan must consider any restrictions or limitations of service disruptions that can result from the test.

- **Security Restrictions**
  The test may require access to confidential data and transactions and sensitive systems and facilities. The BC test plan must consider security policies of the organization, vendors, and alternate recovery facility providers. Appropriate arrangements for security identification cards and authorizations should be made in advance of the test.

- **Length of Time Alternate Recovery Facilities are Available for Testing (Test Period)**
  The length of time available for testing at the alternate recovery facilities is often limited. The reasons for this restriction can vary. Two reasons, for example, are: (1) high rental costs of the facility and (2) prior reservations of the facility by other organizations.

- **Quality of Technical Support**

  A successful test requires highly qualified technical support at the alternate recovery facility but it may not always be available. Consider a test that occurs during peak vacation periods. In this situation, the alternate recovery facility provider may not have sufficient qualified support personnel available to support your test.

- **Space Limitations**

  The physical space allocated at the alternate recovery facilities for testing purposes can be limited. This can restrict the number of teams and team members that can participate in testing at the alternate recovery facilities.

- **Dissimilar Recovery Systems and Equipment**

  Alternate recovery facilities may be equipped with systems and equipment which are different than the systems and equipment at the original site. For example, the alternate recovery facility may contain different versions or configuration of the recovery hardware than the version and configuration deployed at the original site. The test plan needs to address such differences in systems and equipment as testing constraints.

- **Availability of BC Test Teams**

  Availability of team members can become a constraint if the testing period conflicts with the team members' other plans and commitments. Team members, for instance, may have planned vacations or important day-to-day commitments during the test period.

These test constraints provide input into steps 4 to 7 of the framework.

6.5.4 Step 4: Develop Test Strategy

This step defines a strategy to achieve the test objectives defined in Step 2 based on the information from steps 1, 2, and 3. The strategy information related to any current test objectives in previous BC test plans can be used in this step as a basis for developing the current test strategy. This step also ensures that the BC test plan is consistent with the test constraints assessed in Step 3.

The following five components are part of the test strategy:

1. Test timing
2. Test method
3. Test scenario
4. Test evaluation criteria
5. Test spending

These components are described in the sections below.

Test Timing

Establishing a date, time, and duration of the test requires careful consideration of the test constraints and the availability of required resources. Test timing is determined through an evaluation of the readiness and availability of various resources including

1. test software and data,
2. alternate recovery facility vendor,
3. serial numbers and software patches needed for testing the recovery hardware and software,
4. specialized test equipment,
6. BC test teams,

7. recovery hardware, and
8. communication services.

As a general guideline, test timing should minimize impacts to normal business operations and avoid peak workloads, holidays, and important business events.

Test Methods

A number of different test methods were introduced in the first part of this chapter: checklist, walkthrough, simulation, parallel, and full-interruption. The test strategy step selects the most appropriate testing method, and also determines whether the test will be announced or unannounced.

As a general guideline, simple and basic tests should be carried out prior to more complex tests. Checklist testing, for example, is recommended before a walkthrough test; a walkthrough test is recommended before attempting tests such as a simulation or parallel test.

Test Scenario

A test scenario, which is also known as a disruption scenario or disaster scenario, is an essential element of the test strategy. The test scenario describes business disruption conditions in terms of these three components:

1. Type of disruption
2. Disruption narrative
3. Damage caused by the disruption

Type of Disruption

Chapter 2 *Risk Management* includes examples of types of disruptions that businesses can experience. The type of disruption selected to test the business continuity plan must be realistic and credible. A flood scenario, for example, is realistic for businesses that are located close to rivers; similarly, an earthquake scenario is credible for businesses that are near areas which have previously experienced earthquakes, such as California. To add credibility, the type of disruption should correspond to real life events, such as the bombing of the World Trade Center in 2001, major power blackouts of 2003 in USA and Canada, etc.

Disruption Narrative

A disruption narrative describes the business disruption events and conditions related to the test scenario. A disruption narrative includes these two elements: date and time of the disaster, and sequence of events and conditions following the disruption.

1. **The date and time of the disaster**
   The date and time of the disaster helps the BC test teams to assess the possible extent of the resource and data loss, and determine a suitable strategy for recovery. For instance, the teams may conclude that the loss of life is minimal if the disaster occurs during a holiday or during early hours of the morning when no one is on the premises. Moreover, if the company's data was backed up weekly on Fridays and the disaster occurred on a weekend, the teams may determine that no additional transactions need to be applied to the weekly backup to recover the systems. If however, the disaster occurred on a weekday, the teams may determine that additional transactions need to be applied.

2. **Sequence of events and conditions following the disruptive event**

    The disruption narrative should describe the events and conditions triggered by the disaster in sequence. A brief example narrative is as follows: An electrical fire started in the north side of a corporate headquarter building at 10 p.m. on March 18, 2002; Fire trucks arrived at the scene at 10:20 p.m.; By 11 p.m., water from the sprinkler system flooded the computer center located in the building's basement; Management was notified of the event at 10:30 p.m.; and Escalation procedures in the recovery plan were invoked at 10:40 p.m.

Damage Caused by the Disruption

In addition to a disruption narrative, the test scenario provides a description of the internal and external disaster damages to the organization. The description of internal damage to the organization should include impacts to its staff, property, and resources. The internal damage description includes

*   status of all personnel,
*   building safety and operational condition,
*   status of vital records,
*   operational status of IT systems and applications, and
*   impacts to critical business processes.

The description of external damages to the organization can be either local, regional, or national in scope. The external damage description includes information such as

*   areas effected by the disruption;
*   operational status of transportation channels, utilities, communication networks; and
*   impacts to vendors, customers, and suppliers.

Test Evaluation Criteria

Once the test is completed, the results of the test are evaluated based on certain test evaluation criteria. As part of the test strategy, specific evaluation criteria should be developed for the different parts of the business continuity plan being tested. An example of evaluation criteria for a test of the business continuity plan's notification procedures is given below:

1. Was the notification process successful?
2. What was the overall time required to complete the notification procedure?
3. How many team members were contacted?
4. Were the key team members contacted?
5. For those that were not reachable, how many alternates were contacted?
6. How many incorrect phone numbers are on the contact list?
7. How many team members are not on the contact list?

The outcome of this evaluation is a test evaluation report which generally indicates the following:

1. Completion of test objectives
2. Performance of BC test teams
3. Accuracy and validity of the business continuity plan's procedures
4. Adequacy of the recovery resources and facilities
5. Recommendations

The outcome of this phase is a test evaluation report which measures the test successes and failures, and identifies strengths and weaknesses in both the business continuity plan and the test execution. Table 6-1 shows an example outline of a test evaluation report.

	Example Outline of Test Evaluation Report
1	List of successfully completed test objectives
2	List of unsuccessful test objectives, and reasons for their failure
3	List of completed test tasks
4	List of incomplete test tasks
5	Gaps and weaknesses in the BC plan document
6	Performance summary of BC test teams
7	List of problems encountered
8	Adequacy of test resources and recovery facilities
9	Suggestions for improvements for the next test
10	Expense summary
11	Summary of test events in chronological order

Table 6-1: Example outline of test evaluation report

Test Spending Plan

The cost of testing the business continuity plan is mainly driven by the test method and test objectives and scope identified in Step 2. For example, test expenditures are expected to be much higher if the test objectives and test scope require extensive travel and testing to a remote facility, compared with testing at the original site. Examples of common test expenditures are listed below:

- Travel expenses
- Salary expenses for staff and contractors
- Meals and accommodation expenses
- Phone service charges
- Test system and equipment costs
- Alternate recovery facility usage fees
- Backup media shipping costs
- Technical support costs

The test spending plan identifies the expected test expenditures and allocates funds to them. The strategy must ensure the spending plan remains within the overall financial (funding) constraint described in Section 6.5.3 (Step 3 *Assess Test Constraints*).

6.5.5 Step 5: Specify Test Logistics

Military science commonly refers to logistics as the process that deals with the procurement of equipment, mobilization of personnel, and provisioning of facilities as needed for a mission. Logistics also plays a critical role in business continuity plan testing. Test logistics is a process that deals with these four areas:

1. Formation of BC test teams
2. Procurement of test resources and equipment
3. Mobilization of personnel
4. Provisioning of test facilities

Step 5 of the framework specifies the test logistics for these areas based on the test strategy of Step 4 and test constraints of Step 3. The sections below explain the four test logistics areas.

Formation of Business Continuity Test Teams

The BC test teams not only conduct tests, but also participate in test preparation activities. The size, structure, and members of the teams depend on the test method, objectives, and scope. The BC test teams are formed by selecting members of the business continuity teams described in Chapter 5 *Business Continuity Plan Development*. A business continuity team is selected if its roles and responsibilities are essential for achieving the test objectives. Similarly, a business continuity team member is selected if his/her assigned tasks are part of the testing tasks.

BC test teams could also include members that may not be part of the business continuity teams. Below are examples of these additional members:

- **Pre-test Support Personnel**
  These personnel are needed to perform basic pre-test tasks such as shipping and receiving resources and equipment, setup and configuration of the test systems, resources, and facilities.

- **Internal/External Auditors**
  A qualified individual is assigned to audit the test. Their role is to review the test objectives and test plan, monitor and track the test for problems and issues, and create an audit report for management. The report should include impartial findings of test accomplishments, problems and weaknesses, compliance with internal and external guidelines, and recommendations for improvements.

- **Vendors**
  Vendors play a vital support role during the test preparation and test execution phases. Testing relies on vendors for technical support, and services such as installation and configuration of test products and equipment. The test execution phase also provides vendors with an opportunity to identify and fix any limitations of their products and services.

Test Resource Procurement

The resource procurement and logistics team, identified in Chapter 5 *Business Continuity Plan Development*, should be part of any test that requires procurement of resources. Below are some examples of resource procurement activities:

- Order voice and data communication equipment;

- Arrange for a pre-arranged (quick-ship) delivery of computer hardware and software systems;
- Order faxes, printers, copiers, etc.;
- Ensure adequate hardware and software infrastructure is available at the crisis command center, alternate office work area, alternate IT recovery facilities, and alternate manufacturing and production facilities;
- Resolve software license issues with the vendors (e.g. serial number dependencies);
- Arrange technical support from software vendors for test purposes;
- Order backup media;
- Order containers to transport backup media;
- Ensure completeness of backup media inventory;
- Order forms used to track manual procedures;
- Order stationeries, calculators, etc.;
- Ensure availability of test documents including the business continuity plan, and list of inventories;
- Ensure availability of required tools for testing and problem tracking;
- Acquire and install workstations and network infrastructure for alternate office work area.

In order to ensure timely availability of required resources, a detailed list of resource procurement tasks are prepared and executed well in advance of the test date. Advance preparations are a key to minimizing costs and impacts to test timing and schedule which could result from unexpected delays in resource order processing, shipment, and setup.

Mobilization of Personnel

The business continuity plan test generally requires mobilization of BC test teams to remote locations such as off-site storage facilities, alternate IT recovery facilities, alternate manufacturing and production facilities, alternate office work areas, and crisis management center. The resource procurement and logistics team together with the administration support coordination team are responsible for planning and implementing logistics activities to mobilize BC test teams.

The following are examples of logistics activities:

- Determine off-site travel locations.
- Determine who needs to travel to off-site locations.
- Determine when and how long each team member is needed at an off-site location.
- Obtain necessary security approvals to allow team members access to off-site locations.
- Make travel arrangements for team members, including transportation, food, and accommodations.

Certain test constraints, assessed in Step 3, can influence the mobilization of BC test teams. Two examples of such constraints are: (1) travel, food, and accommodation limits specified in the test spending plan (prepared in Step 4 *Develop Test Strategy*); and (2) workspace and workstation capacity limits for test teams at the alternate recovery facilities.

Test Facilities Provisioning

The business continuity test plan includes logistics activities to ensure the availability of test facilities (e.g. alternate recovery facilities) that can adequately support the test requirements. These logistics activities can be divided into three tasks for each alternate recovery facility :

1. Assess Requirements for an Alternate Recovery Facility
2. Assess Current Capabilities of the Alternate Recovery Facility
3. Analyze Requirements and Facility Gaps

Task 1: Assess Requirements for an Alternate Recovery Facility

The first task is to assess the requirements for an alternate recovery facility through a review of the test objectives, test scope, test strategy, and business continuity plan. The following are example requirements for an alternate recovery facility:

1. Type of alternate recovery facility required
2. Test timing and test duration
3. Systems, resources, and equipment needed at the alternate recovery facility
4. Configuration of systems, resources, and equipment needed for the test
5. Technical documentation required for the test
6. Technical support required for the test
7. Voice and data communications requirements for the test

Task 2: Assess Current Capabilities of the Alternate Recovery Facility

The second task is to assess the current capabilities of the alternate recovery facility. The assessment involves two key activities. The first activity requires a careful review of any existing agreements and contracts with the facility owner/vendor. This review for example should determine the following:

1. When and how often the facility can be used for test purposes
2. Procedure for accessing the facility for a test, including the requirements for an advance notice
3. Recovery inventory available for the test at the recovery facility
4. System configuration and capacity of the recovery resources
5. Configuration of the network at the recovery facility
6. Types of manuals and documents available at the recovery facility

7. Extent of the technical support available at the recovery facility
8. Capabilities of voice and data communication services at the recovery facilities
9. Quantity of tape readers for the test

The second activity in the current capabilities assessment involves a visit to the alternate recovery facility. The purpose of the visit is to gain a first-hand understanding of the environment, and to confirm if the facility conforms to the terms of the recovery contract. The visit can focus on the following:

- Recent configuration changes
- Seating and office arrangements
- Telephone facilities
- Security requirements
- Parking facilities
- Building services such as heating, air-conditioning, lighting, restrooms, etc.
- Loading dock locations and procedures
- Multiple clocks providing different time zones and test scenario time
- Network configuration
- Meeting rooms

Task 3: Analyze Requirements and Facility Gaps

The third task in provisioning of a test facility is to perform a gap analysis of the requirements assessed in Task 1 and the current capabilities of the alternate recovery facility determined in Task 2. The gap indicates elements that are missing at the alternate recovery facilities. These gaps are reviewed with the alternate recovery facility vendor and, if required, contracts are amended to ensure that gaps are eliminated.

6.5.6 Step 6: Specify Test Schedule

A test schedule, like any other project schedule, demands careful planning and management. A test schedule details the list of recovery activities, procedures, tasks, priorities, assignments, start and end dates and times, and dependencies. All of the logistical aspects described earlier regarding the BC test teams, resources, and facilities are brought together in a test schedule.

This step can be divided into eight main activities:

1. Review the test objectives and test scope identified in Step 2
2. Review the test constraints assessed in Step 3
3. Select the activities specified in the business continuity plan that are considered relevant for the test based on the review above
4. Select the test logistic activities specified in the test plan
5. Divide the activities from steps 3 and 4 into the three test phases (test preparation, execution, and evaluation)
6. Identify dependencies between test activities
7. Determine the begin and end time for each test activity and their sequence
8. Prepare a test schedule from the results of steps 3 to 5 above

A typical test schedule divides activities into the three business continuity plan testing phases: (1) test preparation phase , (2) test execution phase, and (3) test evaluation phase (see Figure 6-1).

The test preparation phase begins once the BC test plan document is developed. The activities in this phase include pre-test meetings with off-site storage vendors and alternate recovery facility providers. The BC test teams must visit the alternate recovery facilities in order to become familiar with the facility and its equipment, resources, and personnel. Test logistics activities of the BC test plan begin during the test preparation phase.

The actual test is conducted during the test execution phase at the date and time specified by the test plan. This phase covers recovery activities that are part of the test objectives. The test schedule organizes these activities into appropriate recovery categories. Example categories for the IT systems recovery are operating systems recovery activity, applications recovery activities, backup data restoration activities, and IT systems verification activities. The test schedule also includes activities that monitor and track the recovery progress and the performance of BC test teams.

The test evaluation phase begins immediately after the completion of the test execution phase. The test schedule should include activities for evaluating the test results, produce an evaluation report, and present the contents of the evaluation report to management. The purpose these activities is to evaluate the extent of success in achieving the test objectives, team performance, problems encountered during the test, gaps and weaknesses observed in the business continuity plan, and provide recommendations.

6.5.7 Step 7: Identify Test Risks

Minimizing the likelihood of a test failure is the main reason for developing the BC test plan. This step of the framework identifies and controls potential risks of test failures based on a thorough review of all the information gathered in the preceding steps. Below are some examples of review questions to identify potential risks:

- Is the scope of the test too large?
- Does the alternate recovery facility vendor provide adequate technical support for testing?
- Are backup recovery hardware and equipment available in the event of problems with the primary recovery hardware and equipment?
- Has the recovery hardware been pre-configured and tested for compatibility with the original hardware?
- Is the testing team familiar with the alternate recovery facilities?

- Has the backup media been recently verified?
- Does the test plan include sufficient rest time for team members?

Once the risks are identified, they can be ranked in severity as low, medium, and high. Next, the teams should review the risks, determine possible solutions for minimizing the risks, and incorporate the accepted solutions into the BC test plan. The BC test plan should document both the risks and the solutions, which can then be referenced by the test teams during the test preparation and execution phases.

6.5.8 Step 8: Integrate BC Test Plan Components

The results of steps 1 through 7 are integrated in this step to produce the BC test plan document. An example outline of the BC test plan document is given below:

1. BC test plan identification and version number
2. Business continuity plan identification and version number
3. Test sponsor
4. Test date/time
5. Test duration
6. Primary test objectives
7. Secondary test objectives
8. Test scope
9. Test constraints
10. Test method
11. Test scenario(s)
12. Test evaluation criteria
13. BC test teams participating in the test
14. Test resource procurement activities
15. Personnel mobilization activities
17. Provisioning of test facilities

18. Test schedule
    a. Test preparation phase
    b. Test execution phase
    c. Test evaluation phase
19. Test risks
20. Test spending plan

The BC test plan identifier and version number uniquely identify the test plan; the business continuity plan identifier and version number uniquely identify the business continuity plan being tested. The test sponsor indicates the individual(s) who authorize the test.

The remaining elements of the outline consist of information resulting from steps 2 to 7 of the framework. For each element of the outline, Table 6-2 provides a reference to the step name and number in the framework as its main source of information.

Prior to producing a final BC test plan document, the BC test teams must review the contents of the BC test plan for any gaps and inaccuracies. Moreover, team members must have a clear understanding of their individual test related roles and responsibilities. The final BC test plan document becomes a guide for the test preparation, execution, and evaluation phases.

BC Test Plan Outline	Information Source
Test date/time	Step 4: Develop Test Strategy
Test duration	Step 4: Develop Test Strategy
Primary test objectives	Step 2: Identify Test Objectives and Scope
Secondary test objectives	Step 2: Identify Test Objectives and Scope
Test scope	Step 2: Identify Test Objectives and Scope
Test constraints	Step 3: Assess Test Constraints
Test method	Step 4: Develop Test Strategy
Test scenario	Step 4: Develop Test Strategy
Test evaluation criteria	Step 4: Develop Test Strategy
BC test teams participating in the test	Step 5: Specify Test Logistics
Test resource and procurement activities	Step 5: Specify Test Logistics
Personnel mobilization activities	Step 5: Specify Test Logistics
Provisioning of test facilities	Step 5: Specify Test Logistics
Test schedule: • Test preparation phase • Test execution phase • Test evaluation phase	Step 6: Specify Test Schedule
Test risks	Step 7: Identify Test Risks
Test spending plan	Step 4: Develop Test Strategy

Table 6-2: BC test plan outline with reference to information source

Chapter 7
Business Continuity
Plan Maintenance

7.1 Chapter Overview

This chapter examines business continuity plan maintenance, stage 6 of the BCP process. Once the business continuity plan has been tested, the role of the maintenance stage becomes critical. Frequent internal and external changes are common occurrences for businesses. Most of these changes can potentially invalidate the business continuity plan unless it is continually adjusted and modified to reflect these changes.

The objective of this stage is to ensure that the business continuity plan always remains current, complete, accurate, and in a ready-state for execution.

To achieve its objective, the maintenance stage employs the processes

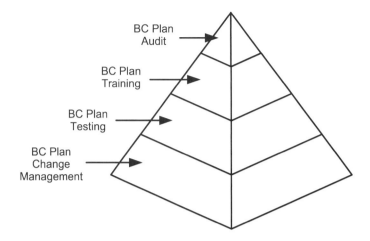

Figure 7-1: BC plan maintenance processes

depicted in Figure 7-1:

1. Business continuity plan change management
2. Business continuity plan testing
3. Business continuity plan training
4. Business continuity plan audits

This chapter describes the role of these processes and concludes with guidelines for maintaining a business continuity plan.

7.2 BC Plan Change Management Process

Without a business continuity plan change management process, business continuity plan maintenance becomes very difficult. A change management process addresses two of the most challenging aspects of plan mainte-nance: monitoring changes in the organization and its external environment; and controlling changes or revisions to the plan. Figure 7-2 shows the

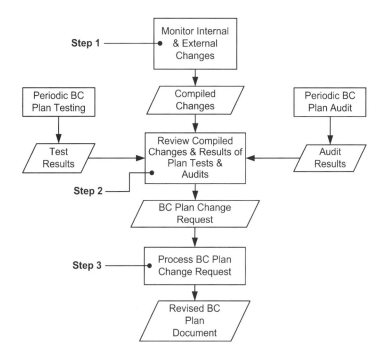

Figure 7-2: BC plan change management process

business continuity change management process. It consists of three main
steps:

    Step 1: Monitor Changes;
    Step 2: Review Compiled Changes, Test Results, and Audit Result; and
    Step 3: Process BC Plan Change Requests.

Changes in the organization and the external environment are monitored in
Step 1; and changes identified as having a potential impact to the business
continuity plan are reviewed in Step 2 to determine if those changes actu-
ally affect the business continuity plan. In Step 2, business continuity plan
change requests are issued for changes that affect the plan. Step 3 pro-

cesses the change requests and updates the plan with necessary changes and revisions. Additional details regarding these steps are described in the sections below.

7.2.1 Step 1: Monitor Changes

Step 1 of the plan's change management process represents the task of constant monitoring of changes in the organization to identify potential impacts to the plan. As depicted in Figure 7-3, changes to the organization can occur at multiple levels: process, people, and resource. Any changes in processes, people, and resources can potentially require changes to certain parts of the plan. For instance, a process-related change can affect recovery priorities; a people-related change can affect business continuity teams or notification procedures; and a resource-related change can affect recovery requirements for IT systems.

A business continuity plan is sensitive to changes that occur not only internally within the organization but those externally in business partners, vendors, alternate recovery facilities, and off-site storage facilities. The

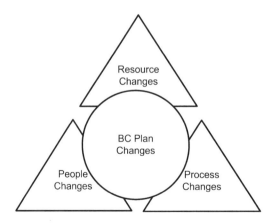

Figure 7-3: Changes impacting the BC plan

examples below demonstrate possible internal and external changes related to processes, people, and resources that may impact the plan.

Process Related Impacts
1. A new strategic product is introduced and as a result new procedures are added to affected business units.
2. A supplier has switched from manually processing orders to automatic order processing using Electronic Data Interchange (EDI).
3. The hot site vendor has introduced a direct 1-800 number to its disaster notification process.

People Related Impacts
1. An early retirement package is given to employees and as a result a number of senior personnel have left the organization.
2. Several key IT technical recovery team members have been promoted to different departments an no longer perform the same roles.
3. The hot site vendor has reorganized its technical support team.

Resource Related Impacts
1. The local area network supporting the organization's critical systems has changed from token-ring to an ethernet architecture.
2. A vendor provides a contracted service to the organization for remote system backups using a proprietary backup and recovery tool. The vendor recently introduced an more efficient version of the tool that automatically detects system configuration changes.
3. The hot site vendor has recently upgraded its mainframe system to accommodate additional customers. This has resulted in certain configuration changes.

The output of this step consists of a compilation of monitored changes that can potentially impact the business continuity plan.

7.2.2 Step 2: Review Compiled Changes, Test Results, and Audit Results

The purpose of this step is to review information that can potentially affect the business continuity plan's accuracy and validity, and cause the organization to issue business continuity plan change requests. There are three main sources of input to this step. The first source of input is the compiled changes resulting from Step 1; the second source is the results of any business continuity plan tests; and the third source is the results of any business continuity plan audits. A change manager, responsible for coordinating the processing of change requests with business continuity teams, reviews the information from these three sources in order to determine if it affects the plan. Following this review, one or more change requests are issued corresponding to the information affecting the plan. These change requests are processed in the Step 3 of the change management process.

7.2.3 Step 3: Process BC Plan Change Requests

This step ensures that updates or revisions to the business continuity plan take place according to the change control procedures specified in the plan. The change request resulting from the preceding step is processed in this step. An example of a high-level procedure for processing a business continuity plan change request is described below. This procedure assumes that there is a change manager with the responsibility to coordinate the processing of the change request with the business continuity teams.

1. Review the change request.
2. Determine nature of the changes required (e.g. people, process, or resource change).
3. Determine the sections or parts of the plan affected by the change.
4. Identify the personnel responsible for the affected areas of the plan who then either create a draft document containing revisions and

changes to their respective areas of the plan or reject the change request related to their part of the plan, and document the reasons.

5. Review all draft documents for any dependencies, conflicts, and inconsistencies; and revise the draft documents if necessary.

6. Finalize the draft documents and obtain approval from authorized personnel.

7. Update the business continuity plan document according to the changes and revisions specified in the approved documents, and apply version controls.

8. Record the changes in this section of the plan.

9. Distribute the business continuity plan to the individuals on the business continuity plan distribution list (see *Business Continuity Plan Distribution List* in Chapter 5, Section 5.14 *BC Plan Appendices*).

7.3 Business Continuity Plan Testing

Business continuity plan testing is the second process used to maintain the business continuity plan. Periodic tests are an excellent opportunity for improving the effectiveness and accuracy of the plan. Test results can reveal the strengths, weaknesses, and gaps of various parts of the plan. For example, periodic plan testing can reveal the following:

- Contact information in the call tree that is not current.
- Vendor contact information that is not up to date.
- Recovery time frames achieved during testing are longer than the recovery time objectives.
- Certain applications failed recovery at test time due to a missing service pack.

The test results also provide an opportunity to determine how well the plan's change management process, as described in the previous section, is implemented. During tests, for instance, discovering that only a few pieces of information are missing in the plan indicates that the change management process is effective.

7.3.1 BC Plan Test Schedule

Establishing a test schedule is an important element of maintaining a business continuity plan. There are two main activities defining a test schedule. The first is to select appropriate test intervals: monthly, quarterly, semiannually, or annually. The second is to assign a test method to each test interval. The assignment of a test method to a test interval should consider the test method's complexity—that is, its testing scope, effort, resources, costs, etc.

Figure 7-4 shows a typical assignment of test methods to a schedule of test intervals and shows their relative complexity. Test methods are represented as circles in the graph. The size of the circles vary, indicating the relative scope of the test method.

Over the entire test schedule of Figure 7-4, the testing begins with the most simple and basic test methods and gradually increases to more complex methods for subsequent tests. Similarly, the test scope is smaller in the beginning and then increases gradually to cover the entire scope of the business continuity plan. In general, the schedule ensures that the tests that occur with greater frequency use simpler methods and scope compared to other less frequent tests. The checklist and walkthrough tests, for instance, are scheduled monthly and quarterly because they are much simpler compared to semiannual or annual tests.

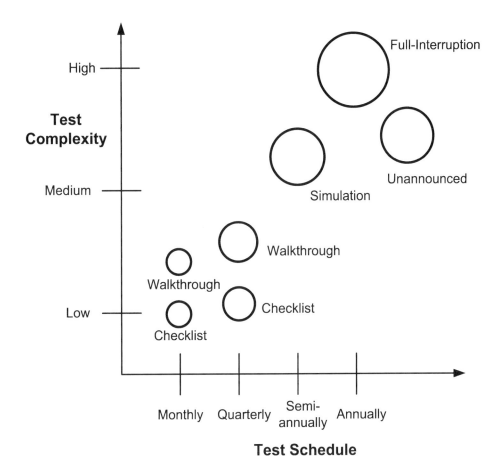

Figure 7-4: Example test schedule in terms of relative test complexity

The following list characterizes the relative complexity of the testing methods in Figure 7-4:

1. **Checklist Test:** low complexity
2. **Walkthrough Test:** low to medium complexity
3. **Simulation Test:** medium to high complexity
4. **Full-interruption Test:** high complexity
5. **Unannounced Test:** medium to high complexity

Using a test schedule, therefore, gradually trains the teams to conduct more complex tests and allows business continuity plan to be completely evaluated. The results and experience from simpler tests are used to improve the business continuity plan and prepare the teams for subsequent more complex tests. The probability of success of a full-interruption test increases considerably as gaps and weaknesses, in both business continuity plan and business continuity test plan, are discovered and addressed in earlier tests.

Testing Intervals

Tests can be conducted at different intervals such as monthly, quarterly, semiannually, or annually. Monthly tests use a checklist or walkthrough method to verify currency and accuracy of the following:

- System and application documents
- Telephone numbers in the contact lists
- Vital records
- Hardware and software inventories
- Vendor contact information
- Product inventories
- Equipment configuration information
- Storage media
- Forms
- Data stored at off-site storage facilities
- Operational manuals

Quarterly tests expand the scope of monthly tests to cover additional areas of the plan such as procedures for

- receiving and responding to the initial disaster event,
- assessing the disaster,

- initiating the business continuity plan,
- notification tasks,
- coordinating business continuity team activities, and
- monitoring recovery and resumption procedures.

The semiannual test uses more advanced test methods such as the simulation test method, and if needed, combines it with a walkthrough and a checklist test method. See Chapter 6 *Business Continuity Plan Testing* for details on test methods. Most areas of the business continuity plan are verified during semiannual testing.

Annual tests, which are typically the most comprehensive in scope, verify all aspects of the business continuity plan. Annual tests are based on either simulation or full-interruption test methods. The scope of the test includes all staff, business units, vendors, business continuity teams, off-site storage facilities, alternate recovery facilities, notification and escalation procedures, recovery and resumptions procedures, etc. The annual test should also exercise the normalization phase in which transition is performed back to the original site or a new cold site from the alternate recovery facility.

7.4 Business Continuity Training

A valid and up-to-date business continuity plan is of little value if the employees responsible for its improvement and execution do not have adequate training and awareness. The business continuity plan maintenance stage implements an enterprise-wide continuous awareness and training program. Management commitment is critical to the success of such a program. Management needs to ensure that a yearly business continuity planning budget includes sufficient funding for training, and ensures that the employees participate in training.

Development of a business continuity awareness and training program is a four step process:

1. Identify awareness and training requirements by specifying who in the organization needs BCP training, and what type of knowledge they need to fulfill their expected roles and responsibilities.

2. Assess the gaps in BCP knowledge between what individuals need and what they currently possess.

3. Select a set of training methods for each individual identified in the requirements, taking into account their training gaps and the training budget.

4. Create a schedule of BCP awareness and training activities using the methods selected above.

Various resources exist for BCP awareness and training, such as

*   internal business continuity policy, brochures, and posters;
*   business continuity plan development, testing, and maintenance activities;
*   BCP events such as seminars and conferences;
*   books and documents covering specific BCP topics;
*   BCP courses,
*   business continuity resources such as BCP organizations and publications (see Appendix B *Business Continuity Resource Information* at the end of this book for a list of BCP resources).

Periodic audits and frequent reviews of the organization's awareness and training program are highly recommended to improve and maintain its quality. To assist with any audits the progress of the organization's awareness and training program should be tracked and documented.

7.5 Business Continuity Audits

Periodic business continuity audits are the fourth important activity of business continuity plan maintenance. A business continuity audit involves an impartial review of organization's business continuity plan and program to determine its compliance with the organization's internal guidelines, and external regulations and standards. The scope of the audit needs to include the all of the stages of the BCP process as described in this book:

1. Risk management
2. Business impact analysis
3. Business continuity strategy development
4. Business continuity plan development
5. Business continuity plan testing
6. Business continuity plan maintenance

From a plan maintenance perspective, gaps and weaknesses in any of the above stages identified in an audit report will result in these activities:

- Redoing those BCP process stages that are identified as having gaps and weaknesses.
- Implementing recommendations of the audit report wherever possible.
- Updating the business continuity plan document to incorporate the changes resulting from the above activities according to the plan's change management process.

7.6 Suggestions for BC Plan Maintenance

Maintaining a business continuity plan document in a constant ready-state is a complex and challenging task. The preceding sections suggested the use of four different processes to help maintain the plan:

1. Business continuity plan change management
2. Business continuity plan testing
3. Business continuity plan training
4. Business continuity plan audits

The list below provides additional suggestions to help maintain the plan:

- Maintain copies of plan in multiple locations such as the primary site, alternate recovery facilities, employees' vehicles and homes, and off-site storage facilities.
- Conduct regular testing to identify gaps and weaknesses in the plan.
- Thoroughly test the plan whenever there are critical changes made to the plan.
- Any significant changes in process, people, or resources should be reviewed for initiating possible plan updates and plan testing.
- Use version control for the business continuity plan and business continuity test plan in order to avoid confusion and use of outdated documents.
- Integrate current and future projects into the BC plan change management process.
- Assign responsibility for business continuity plan maintenance to an experienced person or team.
- Ensure that documented procedures exist for business continuity plan maintenance.
- Ensure that business continuity plan maintenance is part of the annual BCP budget.
- Create an enterprise-wide BCP awareness and training program.
- Create a business continuity plan distribution list that is limited to authorized individuals.
- Adequately train new employees.

Chapter 8
BCP Process: Reports and Documents Summary

By completing all six stages of the BCP process, an organization accumulates crucial information and knowledge—in the form of reports and documents—needed to survive potential disasters or business disruptions. Table 8-1 at the end of this chapter lists the key products of the BCP process.

8.1 Stage 1: Risk Management

The main product of the risk management stage is the risk assessment report which identifies information related to different threats, risks of business losses, and options for controlling risks. The risk assessment report raises the organization's awareness of the possible threats and

potential losses. The report also provides the costs and risk reduction
effectiveness of control options to help management select the most appropriate options.

8.2 Stage 2: Business Impact Analysis

The key product of this stage is the BIA report which identifies critical
business processes, financial and operational impacts from a potential
disaster, and requirements for recovering from a disaster situation. The
BIA report raises management's awareness of those business areas and
resources that are critical for maintaining business continuity. The findings
from the BIA help to define the recovery objectives for the business continuity strategy and the business continuity plan.

8.3 Stage 3: Business Continuity Strategy Development

The outcome of this stage is the business continuity strategy report which
contains viable recovery options for the recovery requirements categorized
into different recovery areas such as work areas, IT systems and infrastructure, manufacturing and production, and critical data and critical/vital
records. The strategy report also provides the cost and capability information for viable recovery options in order to assist management in selecting
the most appropriate recovery option for each recovery requirement.

8.4 Stage 4: Business Continuity Plan Development

The business continuity plan document is the key product of this stage. In the event of a disaster, it is quite possible that the only document that remains safe and available at hand is the business continuity plan. The plan contains all of the key information needed to recover and restore damaged resources and disrupted business processes. It integrates the results of the preceding stages: risk management, business impact analysis, and business continuity strategy development. Table 8-1 lists a typical outline of information required in the business continuity plan.

8.5 Stage 5: Business Continuity Plan Testing

The BC test plan document and test evaluation report are two key outcomes of the business continuity plan testing stage. The BC test plan guides the preparation and execution of the test, while the test evaluation report documents the results of the test once the BC test plan has been executed. The BC test plan also enables an orderly execution of the test, and reduces uncertainties that can hinder the success of the test.

The test evaluation report provides feedback to both management and the BC test teams regarding the results of the test. The report shows how well test objectives were achieved, performance of teams, problems encountered during the test, and gaps and weaknesses observed in the business continuity plan. Table 8-1 includes an example outline of the test evaluation report.

8.6 Stage 6: Business Continuity Plan Maintenance

The following are the key products of the business continuity plan maintenance stage:

- Revised business continuity plan
- Business continuity plan test schedule
- Business continuity training and awareness program
- Business continuity plan audit report

These products are crucial for maintaining the business continuity plan in a constant ready-state for execution. Changes in the organization and the external environment could cause revisions to plan. A test schedule ensures that the plan is tested at regular test intervals and with appropriate test methods to verify the plan's effectiveness and accuracy. A business continuity awareness and training program helps personnel gain the necessary skills required to develop, maintain, and execute the plan. A business continuity plan audit report contains an evaluation of the organization's ability to maintain continuity of business during a disruptive event, and recommends improvements to the company's business continuity program and plan.

BCP Stages	Key Product	Summary of Product Content
Stage 1: Risk Management	Risk Assessment Report	Threats
		Risks
		Critical assets exposed to threats
		For each threat event, a list of control options and their risk control option categories (risk acceptance, risk avoidance, risk reduction, and risk transfer)
		For each risk control option: 1. cost of implementing each risk control option 2. risk reduction effectiveness 3. cost per unit of risk reduction (CURR) 4. the best risk control options based on their CURR values
Stage 2: BIA	BIA Report	Summarized findings such as: 1. Number of business processes and critical business processes for each business function 2. Number of critical business processes reaching their MTDs over a period of time 3. Sum of losses over a period of time
		List of critical business processes
		List of MTDs and criticality rankings
		Prioritized list of systems and applications
		Prioritized list of non-IT resources
		List of recovery point objectives (RPOs)
		List of recovery time objectives (RTOs)
		List of work-around procedures
Stage 3: Business Continuity Strategy Development	Business Continuity Strategy Report	Recovery options for: 1. Work areas 2. IT systems and infrastructure 3. Manufacturing and production 4. Critical data and critical/vital records

Table 8-1: A summary of key products of BCP stages

BCP Stages	Key Product	Summary of Product Content

Stage 4: Business Continuity Plan Development	Business Continuity Plan	1. Objective and scope of the plan
		2. Definition of a disaster
		3. Risk management summary
		4. Summary of business impact assessment
		5. Summary of business continuity strategy
		6. Business continuity teams
		7. Contact information
		8. Activities for BC plan executions phases:
		  a. Initial response and notification
		  b. Problem assessment and escalation
		  c. Disaster declaration
		  d. Plan implementation logistics
		  e. Recovery and resumption
		  f. Normalization
		9. Mapping resources to BC plan execution phases, activities, procedures, and tasks
		10. Assigning activities, procedures, and tasks
		11. BC plan change control management
		12. BC plan appendices

BCP Stages	Key Product	Summary of Product Content

Stage 5: Business Continuity Plan Testing	Business Continuity Test Plan	1. Test plan identifier and version number
		2. BC plan identifier and version Number
		3. Test sponsor
		4. Test date/time
		5. Test duration
		6. Primary test objectives
		7. Secondary test objectives
		8. Test scope
		9. Test constraints
		10. Test method
		11. Test scenario
		12. Test evaluation criteria
		13. BC test teams participating in the test
		14. Test resource and procurement activities
		15. Personnel mobilization activities
		16. Provisioning of test facilities
		17. Test schedule:
		   • Test preparation phase
		   • Test execution phase
		   • Test evaluation phase
		18. Test spending

	Test Evaluation Report	1. A list of successfully completed test objectives 2. A list of unsuccessful test objectives, and reasons for their failure 3. A list of completed test tasks 4. A list of incomplete test tasks 5. Gaps and weaknesses in the BC plan document 6. Performance summary of BC test teams 7. A list of problems encountered 8. Adequacy of test resources and recovery facilities 9. Suggestions for improvements for the next test 10. Expense summary 11. Summary of test events in chronological order

BCP Stages	Key Product	Summary of Product Content
Stage 6: Business Continuity Plan Maintenance	Revised Business Continuity Plan	Business continuity plan revisions and updates.
	Business Continuity Plan Test Schedule	See the product details of Stage 5: business continuity plan testing.
	Business Continuity Awareness and Training Program	Various options for a business continuity awareness and training program are: 1. Internal business continuity policy, brochures, and posters 2. Business continuity plan development, testing, and maintenance activities 3. Business continuity events such as seminars and conferences 4. Books and documents covering specific business continuity topics 5. Business continuity courses 6. Business continuity resources such as business continuity organizations and publications
	Business Continuity Plan Audit Report	An evaluation of an organization's ability to maintain continuity of business during a disruptive event. Compliance with internal and external BCP guidelines. Strengths and weaknesses in the business continuity plan and the six stages of the BCP process.

Appendix A: BCP Standards, Guidelines, and Best Practices

The business continuity community has long recognized the need for a common body of knowledge—standards, guidelines, and best practices—to guide businesses and business continuity professionals to prepare, implement, and maintain business continuity programs. Although international standards that are solely devoted to business continuity planning do not yet exist, a number of organizations have published documents that contribute to the common body of business continuity knowledge. The following are the four key publications that address the topic of business continuity:

- International Standard ISO/IEC 17799:2000—Code of Practice for Information Security Management

- DRI International—Professional Practices for Business Continuity Professionals

- COBIT—Control Objectives for Information and related Technology

- NFPA 1600—Standard on Disaster/Emergency Management and Business Continuity Programs

A.1 International Standard ISO/IEC 17799:2000 Code of Practice for Information Security Management

ISO/IEC 17799 is issued by the International Organization for Standardization (ISO) as a code of practice for information security management. It contains comprehensive guidelines and directions for initiating, implementing, and maintaining information security within an organization.

ISO/IEC 17799 defines security controls for the following ten areas:

- Security Policy
- Organizational Security
- Asset Classification and Control
- Personnel Security
- Physical and Environmental Security
- Communications and Operations Management
- Access Control
- Systems Development and Maintenance
- Business Continuity Management
- Compliance

The *Business Continuity Management* security control addresses guidelines for business continuity. These guidelines cover various aspects of business continuity including

- business continuity management process,
- impact analysis,
- continuity plan development and implementation,
- business continuity planning framework, and
- testing and maintenance of business continuity plans.

ISO/IEC 17799 is based on the Information Security Management Standard BS 7799 published by British Standard Institute in 1995. BS 7799 is divided into two parts:

- BS 7799-1: 1999 Code of Practice for Information Security Management
- BS 7799-2: 2002 Specification for Information Security Management Systems

Part 1 is a guide for initiating, implementing, and maintaining information security. It specifies at a high level what an organization "should" do. The International Standardization Organization has adopted BS 7799 Part 1 as the security standard ISO 17799:2000.

Organizations can use Part 2 to conduct an audit and obtain certification for Information Management Security Systems (ISMS).

A.2 DRI International (DRII)
Professional Practices for Business Continuity
Professionals

DRII was established in 1988 by a group of industry professionals with the objective to

- establish a common base of knowledge (standard) in contingency planning through education, assistance, and publications;
- certify qualified individuals against a minimum acceptable level of measurable knowledge; and
- promote the credibility and professionalism of certified individuals.

In 1997, DRII published a common base of knowledge called "The Professional Practices for Business Continuity Planners". This common base of knowledge has become a part of the industry's best practices standard that outlines the minimum experience required by business continuity professionals. It consists of 10 business continuity subject areas:

- Project Initiation and Management
- Risk Evaluation and Control
- Business Impact Analysis
- Developing Business Continuity Strategies
- Emergency Response and Operations
- Developing and Implementing Business Continuity Plans
- Awareness and Training Programs
- Maintaining and Exercising Business Continuity Programs
- Public Relations and Crisis Communication
- Coordination with Public Authorities

For each subject area, the professional practices for business continuity planners specifies the role of the professional and the recommended knowledge.

DRII has established an on-going process to review its international standard for pertinence and accuracy, and to update the standard accordingly. The standard is used by DRII as a basis for its educational and certification program.

A.3 COBIT

COBIT (Control Objectives for Information and related Technology) is a framework for Information Technology (IT) security and internal controls. This framework is developed by IT Governance Institute as a standard to meet the needs of management to control risks related to information and IT.

COBIT is intended for three types of audiences: management, users, and auditors. It helps management to balance risk with control investments. Users can employ it to obtain assurances on security and control of IT services. Auditors can use it to substantiate their opinion regarding internal controls.

While it serves as a valuable tool for users and auditors, COBIT is primarily a business focused framework containing comprehensive guidance for management and business process owners. Through its control objectives, this framework links IT processes, IT resources, and information to enterprise strategies and objectives. The framework ensures that information and related technology resources that support business objectives are used responsibly, and risks are managed appropriately.

The framework defines 34 high level business control objectives, and their classification structure. The classification structure consists of the following hierarchy:

1   Activities and Tasks: Activities and tasks, at the bottom layer of the hierarchy, are needed to achieve measurable results.

2   Processes: Processes, at the second layer, are defined as series of joined activities or tasks with natural breaks.

3   Domains: At the top layer, processes are grouped into domains to represent the responsibility structure and domains within an organization.

The framework groups IT processes into four domains:

1   Planning and Organization
2   Acquisition and Implementation
3   Delivery and Support
4   Monitoring

A high level business control objective is defined as a business need within a particular IT process. The framework links the high level business control objectives to information criteria and IT resources that are impacted by the objectives. The information criteria is defined in terms of

1   effectiveness,
2   efficiency,
3   confidentiality,
4   integrity,
5   availability,
6   compliance, and
7   reliability.

IT resources are defined in terms of

1 people,
2 applications,
3 technology,
4 facilities, and
5 data.

COBIT addresses business continuity from an IT security perspective. For example, it defines control over the IT process of "Ensuring Continuous Service", classified as part of the Delivery and Support domain. This control has the following characteristics:

- It ensures that IT services are available (as required) and impact to business is minimum in the event of a major disruption.
- It is enabled through an operational and tested IT continuity plan which is in line with the overall business continuity plan.
- It takes into consideration
  a criticality classification;
  b alternative procedures;
  c backup and recovery;
  d systematic and regular testing and training;
  e monitoring and escalation processes;
  f internal and external organizational responsibilities;
  g business continuity activation, fallback and resumption plans;
  h risk management activities; and
  i assessment of single points of failure.

A.4 NFPA 1600
Standard on Disaster/Emergency Management and Business Continuity Programs

NFPA is a nonprofit international organization established in 1896 as the National Fire Protection Association. Its mission is to "reduce the worldwide burden of fire and other hazards on the quality of life by providing and advocating scientifically-based consensus codes and standards, research, training, and education.

On January 14, 2000, NFPA issued NFPA 1600 standard to establish a common set of criteria for disaster management, emergency management, and business continuity programs. On February 11, 2000, the American National Standards Institute (ANSI) endorsed NFPA 1600 as an American National Standard. It is also approved by the Federal Emergency Management Agency (FEMA).

The objective of NFPA 1600 is to provide

- the criteria to assess current disaster, emergency, and business continuity program capabilities; and

- the guidelines to establish a program to mitigate, prepare for, and recover from disasters and emergencies.

NFPA 1600 addresses a wide range of disaster and emergency program elements, including the following:

- Policy
- Program coordination
- Program committee
- Program assessment
- Laws and authorities

- Hazard identification
- Risk assessment
- Hazard mitigation
- Resource management
- Planning
- Direction, control, and coordination
- Communications and warning
- Operations and procedures
- Logistics and facilities
- Training
- Exercises, evaluations, and corrective actions
- Crisis communications
- Public education and information

The standard has evolved from its initial focus on disaster management to a "total program approach"—that combines disaster/emergency management planning and business continuity program in both private and public sectors. The current version of the standard represents a coordinated effort of the representatives from the Federal Emergency Management Agency, the National Emergency Management Association, and the International Association of Emergency Managers.

Appendix B: Business Continuity Resource Information

B.1 Business Continuity Planning Related Organizations

Business Continuity Planners Association (BCPA)
(www.bcpa.org)

The Business Continuity Planners Association (BCPA) is a nonprofit association with the mission to provide an environment to exchange professional and educational information and experiences related to business recovery, crisis management, emergency management, contingency planning, disaster preparedness, or a related professional vocation.

Disaster Recovery Institute International (DRII)

(www.drii.org)

DRI International was founded in 1988 by a group of professionals that forecasted the demand for comprehensive business continuity education. DRII provides a global certification program for business continuity/disaster recovery planners. In 1997, DRII and the Business Continuity Institute published the "Professional Practices for Business Continuity Planners" as the industry's common base of knowledge. It also offers business continuity and disaster recovery training courses.

Business Continuity Institute

(www.thebci.org)

The Business Continuity Institute (BCI) was established in 1994 with the mission to promote the art and science of business continuity management. With its 1450 members in 41 countries, BCI promotes the highest standards of professional competence and commercial ethics in the provision and maintenance of business continuity management services. Its aim is to define professional competencies for business continuity professionals, provide an internationally recognized certification program, and promote continuous professional development for maintaining professional competencies.

British Standards Institute (BSI)

(www.bsi-global.com)

Established in 1901, BSI is the national standard body of United Kingdom. One of its main responsibilities includes facilitating, drafting, publishing, and marketing British Standards and other guidelines. BSI addresses business continuity planning in the BS 7799 standard which consists of two parts: part 1, BS 7799-1: 1999 Code of Practice for Information Security Management; and part 2, BS 7799-2: 2002 Specification for Information Security Management Systems (ISMS). Part 1 of BS 7799 has been adopted as an international standard (ISO/IEC 17799).

Information Systems Audit and Control Association (ISACA)
(www.isaca.org)

ISACA is a global organization serving as a centralized source of information and guidance for information governance, control, security and audit professionals. ISACA has been actively publishing IS auditing and IS control standards and guidelines which are followed by professionals worldwide. IT Governance Institute, which is affiliated with ISACA, is responsible for publishing COBIT (Control Objectives for Information and related Technology) as a framework for Information Technology (IT) security and internal controls. One of the control objectives within COBIT deals with the topic of business continuity.

Survive—The Business Continuity Group
(www.survive.com)

Survive was established in 1981 as a business continuity group with the objective to provide a forum for exchange of information, ideas, and experiences among business continuity professionals. To achieve its objective, Survive publishes a magazine and holds conferences, meetings, and workshops.

The Association of Contingency Planners (ACP)

(www.acp-international.com)

The Association of Contingency Planners (ACP) is a nonprofit association founded in 1983. It promotes an environment for international
networking and information exchange related to contingency and
business resumption planning. ACP issues a quarterly corporate news-
letter entitled 'The ACP Sentinel', which includes business reports,
announcements, and planned activities. ACP enables its members to
learn about state-of-the-art contingency and business continuity tech-
niques through educational programs at the chapter and corporate
levels.

Securities Industry Association's Business Continuity Planning Committee

(www.sia.com)

The disaster of September 11, 2001 prompted the creation of SIA's
Business Continuity Planning Committee in October 2001. Its objective is to provide a forum for securities firms, industry organizations,
and service providers to share specific plans and business continuity
information. The committee is currently divided into nine subcommit-
tees: SIA BCP Command Center, Exchange/Markets, Utilities &
Service Providers, Critical Physical Infrastructure and Urban Renewal,
Best Practices, Insurance, Catastrophic Events, Industry Testing, and
Regional Issues.

Disaster Recovery Information Exchange (DRIE)

(www.drie.org)

Established in 1994, DRIE aims to become the primary source of
information and education for contingency planners. It is a Canada-

wide organization with chapters in various Canadian cities. DRIE and its chapters organize regular conferences and seminars on the subject of disaster recovery and contingency planning.

American Red Cross
(www.redcross.org)

American Red Cross Services responds to disasters that cause human suffering or create human needs. Its mission is to ensure nationwide disaster planning, preparedness, community disaster education, mitigation, and response.

Canadian Centre for Emergency Preparedness
(www.ccep.ca)

The Canadian Centre for Emergency Preparedness (CCEP) is a non-profit organization with objective to raise awareness of the risk of disasters and promote disaster management to individuals, communities, and organizations within Canada. It aims to achieve its objective through activities such as promotion of sound disaster management principles and practices, education and training, career development, research, and services and products. CCEP holds an annual World Conference on Disaster Management.

Federal Emergency Management Agency (FEMA)
(www.fema.gov)

FEMA is an independent agency of the U.S. federal government, established in 1979. Its mission is to reduce loss of life and property and protect the nation's critical infrastructure from all types of hazards. FEMA adopts a comprehensive, risk-based, emergency management program of mitigation, preparedness, response and recovery. FEMA has developed an "Emergency Management Guide" for business and industry to help with emergency planning, response, and recovery.

International Disaster Recovery Association (IDRA)

(www.idra.com)

IDRA was established in 1989 with a focus on voice, data, image, and sensory telecommunications aspects of Disaster Recovery Planning (DRP), Contingency Planning, and Business Continuation. It also has another IDRA special interest group (SIG) that concentrates on security, terrorism, employee safety and workplace violence. It holds an annual conference that covers topics such as contingency planning, risk management, voice, data, image or sensory telecommunications, corporate security, international management, management information systems, emergency management, executive protection, and public safety.

National Fire Protection Agency (NFPA)

(www.nfpa.org)

NFPA is a nonprofit organization focused on reducing the worldwide burden of fire and other hazards on the quality of life. It issues safety codes and standards, provides education to protect life and property, and promotes professional development and certification programs. NFPA 1600 is a standard issued by NFPA for Disaster/Emergency Management and Business Continuity Programs—to guide the private and public sector in the development of a program for effective disaster preparedness, response, and recovery.

International Organization for Standardization (ISO)
(www.iso.org)

ISO is the world's largest developer of standards, having developed more than 14000 international standards for business, government, and society. ISO represents a bridge between public and private sectors through a network of national standards institutes from 147 countries working in partnership with international organizations, governments, industry, business and consumer representatives. ISO has developed a number of standards that address business continuity and risk management.

The Natural Hazards Center
(www.colorado.edu/hazards)

The Natural Hazards Center, associated with the University of Colorado, in Boulder, Colorado, USA, has the objective to disseminate information and increase communication among individuals, researchers, agencies, and organizations actively working to reduce disaster damage and suffering. It provides information on natural hazards and human adjustments to hazards and disasters through annual workshop, research, library services, and on-line resources.

The Financial Services Technology Consortium (FSTC)
(www.fstc.org)

FSTC is a consortium of leading North American-based financial institutions, technology vendors, independent research organizations, and government agencies. It aims to promote interoperable, open-standard technologies to support critical infrastructure for the financial services industry. The FSTC has a number of Standing Committees to address key financial service technology areas, one of which deals with business continuity for financial services industry.

The Association of Insurance and Risk Managers (AIRMIC)

(www.airmic.com)

AIRMIC is a UK based organization dedicated to the field of insurance and risk management. AIRMIC supports its members with self-development, technical awareness, and internal working relationships. Together with the Institute of Risk Management (IRM) and ALARM The National Forum for Risk Management in the Public Sector, AIRMIC has formulated a new Risk Management Standard.

B.2 Natural Hazard and Disaster Information

United Nations Environment Programme (UNEP)

(www.grid.unep.ch/activities/earlywarning/preview)

Through its project of Risk Evaluation, Vulnerability, Information & Early Warning, UNEP has developed an online tool to visualize data on worldwide natural disasters.

USGS—U.S. Geological Survey

(www.usgs.gov)

USGS is a federal source for science about the Earth, its natural and living resources, natural hazards, and the environment. The Earthquake Hazard program of USGS provides an online map and a list of last 8 to 30 days of worldwide earthquake activities (earthquake.usgs.gov/recenteqsww).

Incident.com
(www.incident.com)

This website displays a map of recent hazards and disaster events built on-the-fly from Internet data sources.

Federal Aviation Administration (FAA)
(www.faa.gov)

FAA's website provides access to preliminary accident and incident data that has been received by the Office of Accident Investigation during the last 10 business days.

Federal Emergency Management Agency (FEMA)
(www.fema.gov/news/disasters.fema)

FEMA's website maintains a library of major US disaster declarations.

American Red Cross
(www.redcross.org/news)

The American Red Cross provides access to their news articles related to recent disaster events on their website.

Department of Geology, University of California Davis
(www-geology.ucdavis.edu/eqmandr.html)

The department of geology's website contains recent earthquake information.

University of Edinburgh
(www.geo.ed.ac.uk/quakes/quakes.html)

University of Edinburgh's website supports an online worldwide earthquake locator.

US Environmental Protection Agency (EPA)
(www.epa.gov/epahome/commsearch.htm)

EPA's website contains a database of environmental facts such as pollution, hazardous waste sites, and other regulatory information. The database supports a zip code based search of environmental information about a specific location and community.

NOAA Satellite and Information
National Environmental Satellite, Data, and Information Service (NESDIS)
(www.nesdis.noaa.gov)

NOAA's website provides timely access to global environmental data and imagery—from satellite and other sources—for various hazards such as dust storms, fires, floods, icebergs, ocean, and severe weather.

B.3 List of BC Related Publications

- Contingency Planning and Management
  (www.contingencyplanning.com)

- Disaster Recovery Journal
  (www.drj.com)

- Continuity Insights Magazine
  (www.continuityinsights.com)

- Disaster Prevention and Management
  (www.emeraldinsight.com)

- Disaster Recovery Yellow Pages
  (www.disaster-help.com)

- Hazardous Material Management Magazine
  (www.hazmatmag.com)

- Risk Management Magazine
  (www.rmmag.com)

- Information Security Magazine
  (infosecuritymag.techtarget.com)

- Business Continuity Magazine
  (www.kablenet.com/bc)

- NFPA Journal
  (www.nfpa.org)

Glossary of BCP Terms and Abbreviations

Acquire-as-needed

Recovery option in which critical IT and non-IT resources are acquired from a supplier based on the need following a disruption *(see also pre-established, pre-arranged (quick-ship))*.

Alternate office work area

An alternate facility containing office equipment and resources (such as desks, telephones, personal computers, fax and copier machines, etc.) needed for staff to perform their office work during the recovery period following a business disruption *(see also crisis management center, and work area)*.

Alternate IT recovery facility

An alternate facility where IT systems and infrastructure are recovered in the event of a disruption to the primary facility.

Alternate manufacturing and production facility

An alternate facility where manufacturing and production equipment are recovered in the event of a disruption to the primary facility.

Alternate recovery facility

Refers to an alternate IT recovery facility, an alternate manufacturing and production facility, or a work area.

Announced test

Business continuity plan test that is announced to teams prior to execution.

BSI

British Standards Institute

BS 7799

Information Security Management Standard published by British Standard Institute. The standard contains two parts:
- BS 7799-1: 1999 Code of Practice for Information Security Management, and
- BS 7799-2: 2002 Specification for Information Security Management Systems.

Business continuity planning process (BCP process)

Defines a life cycle for developing and maintaining a business continuity plan. The BCP process life cycle consists of six phases: risk management, business impact analysis, business continuity strategy development, business continuity plan development, business continuity plan testing, and business continuity plan maintenance.

Business continuity planning management (BCP management)

Focuses on management and organizational activities related to business continuity planning, such as developing and implementing a business continuity policy, establishing a BCP steering committee, initiating a plan development project, ensuring compliance with laws and regulations, etc.

Business continuity coordinator (BCC)

A person who has an overall responsibility for managing the business continuity plan through its phases of development, testing, maintenance and execution. During the plan execution phase, the BCC coordinates the plan execution activities and provides a critical communication link between CMT and other business continuity teams.

Business continuity planning (BCP)

Business continuity planning is a discipline that prepares an organization to maintain continuity of business during a disaster through an implementation of a business continuity plan *(see also BCP management, and BCP process)*.

Business continuity plan (BC plan)

A document containing procedures and guidelines to help recover and restore disrupted processes and resources to normal operational status within an acceptable time frame following a disaster or a disruptive event.

Business continuity teams

Teams responsible for development, maintenance, testing, and execution of the business continuity plan.

Business continuity test teams (BC test teams)

Teams responsible for testing the business continuity plan.

Business impact analysis (BIA)

A BIA is a process that determines the financial and operational impact of a disruption to a business, and the requirements for recovering from the disruption.

Business continuity plan execution phases

Business continuity plan is executed in phases which consist of initial response and notification, problem assessment, disaster declaration, plan implementation logistics, recovery and resumption, and normalization phases.

Business continuity strategy

Business continuity strategy is composed of a set of recovery options that are utilized as alternatives in the event that existing critical resources are unavailable.

Business disruption

(see disaster)

Business function

An area of business responsible for one or more related business processes needed to support company's mission.

Business process

Business process defines one or more related tasks or activities of a business function.

Call tree

A hierarchical structure containing information about the business continuity team members and their notification sequence *(see also contact list)*.

Checklist test

A basic business continuity plan test method that reviews the BC plan to determine the currency and adequacy of the resources and components specified in the plan.

Cold site

An alternate recovery facility that does not have any recovery resources and infrastructure such as hardware, software, or data and voice communications equipment. A cold site may include basic services such as power, heating, air-conditioning, water, sprinkler systems, and raised floors for computing equipment *(see also warm site, and hot site)*.

Contact list

A contact list contains information on how to contact each BCP team member such as team member name, telephone number, email address, etc. *(see also call tree)*.

Critical business process

A business process that is critical for maintaining business continuity.

Critical IT resources

IT systems and applications that support critical business processes.

Critical non-IT resources

Non-IT resources used to support critical business processes.

Crisis communication plan

A crisis communication plan guides the crisis management team in providing timely, consistent, and accurate crisis information to the personnel within the organization, business partners, customers, and the public.

Crisis management center (CMC)

A facility where the crisis management team can conduct recovery efforts *(see also work area, and office work area).*

Critical data

Critical data can include critical IT applications and components needed to support those applications, such as operating systems, databases, and data (see also critical record, and vital record).

Critical record

Critical records are used by critical processes for legal, regulatory, and operational purposes. Critical records include information contained in documents, drawings, and photographs, etc. *(see also critical data, and vital record).*

DRII

(Disaster Recovery Institute International)

Detailed problem report

A detailed problem report is produced during the problem assessment phase, phase 2 of the business continuity plan execution phases. This report provides an overview of the cause and extent of damage.

Disaster

An event that disrupts critical business processes and degrades their service levels to a point where the resulting financial and operational impact to an organization becomes unacceptable.

Disaster declaration statement

A statement that officially declares a disaster event according to the disaster declaration definitions and procedures specified in the business continuity plan.

Disruption

(see disaster)

Disruptive event

(see disaster)

Emergency response plan

An emergency response plan contains guidelines and procedures to follow immediately after a disaster in order to prevent loss of life and injuries and minimize damages to the organization's assets.

FEMA

(Federal Emergency Management Association)

Financial impact

Financial impact measure the extent and severity of financial loss to the business in the event of a disruption.

Full-interruption test

A full-interruption test activates all components of the business continuity plan and assumes all critical business processes are disrupted. In addition, it can interrupt normal business operations.

Hot site

An alternate facility that contains pre-configured hardware, software, data and voice communications infrastructure needed for recovering critical business processes *(see also cold site, and warm site)*.

ISO (International Organization for Standardization)

ISO, a network of national standards institutes of 148 countries, is the world's largest developer of technical standards. It has issued standards such as ISO 9000, ISO 14000, and ISO/IEC 17799.

ISO/IEC 17799

Code of practice for information security management. It contains comprehensive guidelines and directions for initiating, implementing, and maintaining information security within an organization (see also BS 7799).

Lost data

The data which is lost between the time of the last backup of data and the business disruption event *(see also work backlog)*.

NFPA (National Fire Protection Association)

A nonprofit organization with a focus on reducing the worldwide burden of fire and other hazards on the quality of life. It is responsible for developing the NFPA 1600 standard for disaster/emergency management and business continuity programs.

NFPA 1600

A standard for disaster/emergency management and business continuity programs issued by NFPA and endorsed by FEMA.

Off-site data storage facility

An alternate facility where copies of the critical data are stored. In the event of a disruption, the stored critical data is retrieved from the alternate facility and used during recovery *(see also off-site storage facility, and off-site record storage facility)*.

Off-site record storage facility

An alternate facility where copies of the critical and vital records are stored. In the event of a disruption, the stored records are retrieved from the alternate facility and used to recover from the disruption *(see also off-site storage facility and off-site data storage facility)*

Off-site storage facility

A facility where the copies of the critical data, critical records, and vital records can be stored *(see also off-site data storage facility, and off-site record storage facility)*.

Operational impact

Operational impact is a negative effect of a disruption on various qualitative aspects of business operations, such as efficiency, satisfaction, image, confidence, and control.

Original facility

A facility which a business uses to conduct its normal business operations. In order to differentiate it from an alternate recovery facility, this facility is described in various terms such as original facility or site, primary facility or site, and damaged facility or site.

Parallel test

In this test, systems are recovered at the alternate recovery facility using the last backup of data while the production environment continues to function as normal. Any transactions at the production environment are recorded manually and reentered into recovered systems at the alternate recovery facility. At the end of the test the state of both environments at the alternate recovery facility and original facility are compared.

Pre-arranged (quick-ship)

A recovery option in which an agreement is made with a vendor that guarantees the delivery of systems or equipment (needed for recovering from a disruption) within an agreed time following a disruption *(see also pre-established, and acquire-as-needed)*.

Pre-established

A recovery option in which alternate systems and equipment—
needed for recovering from a disruption—are acquired and installed
at an alternate recovery facility prior to a disruption event (*see also*
pre-arranaged(quick-ship), and acquire-as-needed).

Preliminary problem report

Preliminary problem report is produced during the initial response
and notification phase, phase 1 of the business continuity plan
execution phases. This report provides an overview of the cause
and extent of the damage.

Maximum tolerable downtime (MTD)

Length of time a process can be unavailable before the company
experiences significant losses. MTD corresponds to time period
between the disruptive event and start of normal processing.

Simulation test

In this test, business disruption is simulated and business continuity
test teams executes tasks and procedures specified in one or more
parts of the business continuity plan. Some tasks and procedures
may be simulated to minimize the cost and interruptions to normal
business operations.

Recovery areas

Areas of business with critical resources that need to be recovered
in the event of a business disruption. Typical recovery areas include
IT systems and infrastructure, manufacturing and production, work
areas, and critical data and critical/vital records.

Recovery option

An alternative option for recovering disrupted critical resources.
For example, a cold site, warm site, and hot site are three options
for recovering IT systems and infrastructure.

Recovery point objective (RPO)

Refers to the tolerance for the loss of data measured in terms of the time between the last backup of data and the disaster event. RPO is an indicator of how much lost data can be recovered once systems are recovered and updated with the last backup of data.

Recovery priority

Sequence for recovering critical business processes.

Recovery time objective (RTO)

Length of time available for recovering disrupted systems and resources.

Recovery time requirements

Time frames that collectively represent the requirements to recover from a disruption, such as Maximum Tolerable Downtime (MTD), Recovery Time Objective (RTO), Recovery Point Objective (RPO), and Work Recovery Time (WRT).

Risk

A chance or likelihood of a threat source causing an event with adverse business impacts.

Risk acceptance

Risk control option which accepts the risk of a threat as tolerable and does not require additional steps to reduce or eliminate the risk.

Risk assessment

Risk assessment is a process that begins with the identification of potential threats to an organization and ends with a set of risk values for those threats.

Risk avoidance

Risk control option which avoids the risk altogether.

Risk control option

Options for controlling the risks of threats. Risk control options can be divided into four areas: risk acceptance, risk avoidance, risk reduction, and risk transfer.

Risk mitigation

Risk control option which reduces the risk to an acceptable level.

Risk transfer

Risk control option which transfers the risk to another entity or organization (e.g. an insurance company).

Threat event

A disruptive event caused by a threat source (e.g. a power outage event caused by an ice storm - a threat source).

Threat source

The source of a threat event. (e.g. an ice storm can be a source of a power outage - a threat source).

Unannounced test

Business continuity plan test which is initiated without a prior announcement of the test to the BC test team.

Vital records

Critical records that are either irreplaceable, or difficult or expensive to reproduce *(see also critical data, and critical record)*.

Walkthrough test

Business continuity test teams meet to verbally walkthrough the activities, procedures, and tasks they are expected to follow during the execution of the business continuity plan. This test allows the members of business continuity test teams to review and critique each others' test activities and performance. It is also known as a tabletop test.

Warm site

An alternate recovery facility containing some of the required hardware, software, machinery, equipment, and data and voice communications infrastructure that must be prepared and configured for recovery activities following a business disruption. A full recovery requires additional systems and equipment at a warm site *(see also cold site, and hot site)*.

Work-around procedure

Alternate procedures for handling work and processing transactions in the event of a disruption to normal procedures.

Work backlog

Work collected manually between the time of the disruption event and systems/resource recovery *(see also lost data)*.

Work area

Alternate office work area or crisis management center or both *(see also office work area, crisis management center, and recovery areas)*.

Work recovery time (WRT)

Length of time needed to recover lost data, work backlog, and manually captured work once systems/resources are recovered and repaired. WRT corresponds to the time between systems/resource recovery and the start of normal processing.

References

1 Random House Webster's College Dictionary, Random House Inc., New York, 1997.
2 V. Wheatman, After Math: Disaster Recovery, Gartner Research, AV-14-5238, September 2001.
3 New Insights into Business Continuity for Financial Institutions, White Paper, Sungard Recovery Services LLP, November 2001.
4 C. Jackson, CSI Checklist: How the September 11 Attack Should Impact Your Continuity Planning, Computer Security Journal, Volume XVIII, Number 1, 2002.
5 Janette Ballman, Merrill Lynch Resumes Business Critical Functions Within Minutes of Attack, Disaster Recovery Journal, Fall 2001.
6 Anti-Bribery and Books & Records Provisions of The Foreign Corrupt Practices Act, Pub. L. 105-366, November 10, 1998.
7 Gramm-Leach-Bliley Act, PUBLIC LAW 106–102—NOV. 12, 1999.

8 Comptroller of the Currency, Administrator of National Banks, Banking Circular 177 (Revised), July 12, 1989 (Revised).

9 Comptroller of the Currency, Administrator of National Banks, Banking Circular 187, Jan 18, 1985.

10 FFIEC, Interagency statement, Guidance Concerning Contingency Planning in Connection with Year 2000 Readiness, May 13, 1998.

11 Computer Security Act of 1987, Public Law 100-235 (H.R. 145), January 8, 1988.

12 Electronic Fund Transfer Act, Pub. L. No. 90-321, May 29, 1968.

13 JCAHO Requirement, Emergency Management Standards, EC.1.4 and EC.2.9.1, January 2001.

14 M. Swanson, A. Wohl, L. Pope, T. Grance, J. Hash, R. Thomas, Contingency Planning Guide for Information Technology Systems, NIST Special Publication 800-34.

15 PDD 67, Enduring Constitutional Government and Continuity of Operations, October 21, 1998.

16 Business Continuity Institute, and D. Smith, Business Continuity and Crisis Management, Management Quarterly, The Institute of Chartered Accountants of England and Wales, January 2003.

17 NFPA 1600, Standard on Disaster/Emergency Management and Business Continuity Programs, NFPA, January 14, 2000.

18 D. Scott, Best Practices and Trends in Business Continuity Planning, Gartner Symposium, ITXPO, October 2002.

19 Business Continuity Planning Model, DRI International, http://www.drj.com/new2dr/model/bcmodel.htm.

20 P. Kilbridge, M.D., Computer Crash – Lessons from a System Failure, NEJM (Medical Journal), Volume 348:881-882, Number 10, March 6, 2003.

21 FEMA, which is the Federal Government's executive agent for COOP, provides COOP guidance in FPC 65, Federal Executive Branch Continuity of Operations.

22 ISO/IEC 17799:2000, Information Security - Code of Practice for Information Security Management, International Organization for Standardization, 2000.

23 M. Bland, Communicating out of a Crisis, Macmillan Press Ltd, London, 1998.

24 J. W. Toigo, Disaster Recovery Planning: Strategies for Protecting Critical Information, Prentice Hall PTR, Upper Saddler River New Jersey, 2nd Edition, 2000.

25 K. Tilley, Work-Area Recovery Planning: the key to coporate survival, Business Continuity, July 1995, pp. 18-21.

26 R. Bates, Disaster Recovery Planning, McGraw-Hill, 1991.

27 J. Toigo, Disaster Recovery Planning, 1989.

28 P. Corrigan, Planning for Disaster, LAN Times, July 25, 1994.

29 L. Wrobel, Write a Great Disaster Plan, Network Computing, March 1994.

30 National Institute of Standards and Technology, SP 800-30, Risk Management Guide, June 2001.

31 D. Hayward, A Disaster Waiting to Happen, CUA Userlink, V3 i2, March 1994.

32 R. Heath, Crisis Management for Managers and Executives, Financial Times Pitman Publishing, London, 2000.

33 V. Lloyd, Business Continuity Planning, a Waste of Money or a Benefit?, Business Continuity, Sept 1993, p20-21, ISSN.

34 M. Pember, Information disaster planning: An integral component of corporate risk management, Records Management Quarterly, April, 1996, pp.31-37.

35 C. Cappelletti, Designing and Implementing a Disaster Recovery Plan, SANS Institute, 2001.

36 J. Girard, Disaster Management Plan for Remote Access, TG-14-5458, Research Note, Gartner Inc., 2001.

37 F. Luevano, How E-Business Is Changing Business Continuity Programs. Best Practices & Case Studies, Note QA-13-8626, Gartner, Inc., 2001.

38 K. N. Myers, Manager's Guide to Contingency Planning for Disasters: Protecting Vital Facilities and Critical Operations, J. Wiley & Sons, 1999.

39 R. Witty, Integrating BCP Into the IT Project Life Cycle, TU-13-8386, Research Note, Gartner Inc. 2001.

About the Authors

Dr. Akhtar Syed, Ph.D., CISSP

Dr. Syed has extensive training and consulting experience in the field of Business Continuity Planning (BCP). As a consultant and trainer, he has assisted numerous organizations with BCP training, business impact analysis, continuity strategy assessment, and business continuity plan development and testing. He has also worked with IBM Global Services as a senior business continuity consultant, helping businesses with alternate disaster recovery facility solutions.

Dr. Syed holds a doctorate degree in systems design engineering, masters degree in the field of data communication services, and a bachelors degree in computer science. He is also a Certified Information Systems Security Professional (CISSP).

Afsar Syed, BMath., ABCP

Afsar is a senior business continuity consultant, and has over 15 years of progressive business and technical experience in telecommunications, wireless and wireline data networking, voice over IP services, Internet security, database systems, computer programming, and product and project management. He possesses a bachelor of mathematics degree in computer science and is an Associate Business Continuity Professional (ABCP).

Index

W

www.sentryx.com

Business Continuity Training

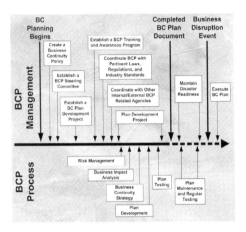

BUSINESS CONTINUITY PLANNING
(5-day BC-201)

Now includes BC-301
Advanced BIA on day 3

Course Information

This course is available for on-site and off-site training.

The course fee is $2000 USD. Package pricing and discounts are available for multiple enrollments.

About Sentryx

Sentryx is dedicated to providing professional business continuity training and consulting services.

Our course instructors are experienced business continuity professionals with industry designations from DRI International and ISC².

For more information on business continuity training and consulting services, email us at **info@sentryx.com** or visit our web site at **www.sentryx.com** or call **1-800-869-8460**.

Features

- A step-by-step methodology to help you implement a business continuity program and develop, test, and maintain a business continuity plan.

- Detailed analysis and steps for conducting a business impact analysis, managing risks, and developing a business continuity strategy.

- A comprehensive overview of the business continuity planning principles and guidelines.

- Protection and recovery of the key aspects of business such as mission critical business processes, IT systems and infrastructure, manufacturing and production equipment and products, facilities, work areas, vital records, critical data, and services.

Audience

This course is designed for anyone responsible for developing business continuity plans, managing business continuity projects, or participating in business continuity planning.

The course is especially useful for business continuity planners, business unit managers, project managers, senior management, and staff from information technology, security, emergency response, communications, and human resource departments.

It is an excellent resource for people seeking certifications such as CISSP (Certified Information Systems Security Professional) or CBCP (Certified Business Continuity Professional).

Description

This course teaches the principles of Business Continuity Planning (BCP) and provides the skills needed to develop a business continuity plan.

The course is based on industry best practices and guidelines for the six stages of the BCP process:

- Risk management
- Business impact analysis
- Business continuity strategy development
- Business continuity plan development
- Business continuity plan testing
- Business continuity plan maintenance

The steps required to implement each of these stages are explored in detail and specific examples are used throughout the course to reinforce BCP concepts.

Students gain skills through discussions, hands-on practice in small group exercises, and through an easy to follow student manual.

Visit www.sentryx.com for a list of all courses.

www.sentryx.com

BCKnowledge Pro™ Computer-based Business Continuity Training

...helping businesses maintain continuity.

Comprehensive, practical, and effective business continuity training at your own pace and convenience.

BCKnowledge Pro™ is an innovative computer-based Business Continuity training package designed to teach principles, concepts, and practical methods needed to develop, test, and maintain a business continuity plan and a business continuity program. The objective of BCKnowledge Pro™ is to provide students with practical, detailed understanding and knowledge of Business Continuity and to help students prepare their organizations to deal with potential business disruptions and disaster situations.

Through its interactive capabilities along with quizzes and exercises, BCKnowledge Pro™ provides students an exciting, fun, and practical way of learning Business Continuity. With the help of its unique design and state-of-the-art multimedia learning technology, BCKnowledge Pro™ closely resembles instructor-led Business Continuity courses. Unlike instructor-led Business Continuity courses, BCKnowledge Pro™ allows students to learn at their own pace and on their own schedule.

For more information on business continuity training services, email us at info@sentryx.com or visit our web site at www.sentryx.com.

BCKnowledge Pro™ is designed for all employees at all levels of the organization including general company staff, business continuity practitioners, IT staff, business continuity coordinators, auditors, and senior and executive management. This package is structured in a series of courses that cover an extensive range of topics. The modular structure of BCKnowledge Pro™ gives students the flexibility to take either all courses or only specific courses depending on their training requirements.

BCKnowledge Pro™ includes 8 courses:
- BCK101 Business Continuity Planning 1
- BCK102 Business Continuity Planning 2
- BCK200 Business Continuity Management
- BCK301 Risk Management
- BCK302 Business Impact Analysis
- BCK303 Business Continuity Strategy Development
- BCK304 Business Continuity Plan Development
- BCK305 Business Continuity Plan Testing and Maintenance

Features
- Interactive multimedia based lectures that include audio, video, text, and dynamic illustrations
- Practical examples reinforce business continuity concepts
- Full glossary of business continuity terms and definitions including terminologies such as disaster, business function, business process, Maximum Tolerable Downtime (MTD), Recovery Time Objective (RTO), Recovery Point Objective (RPO), etc.
- Quizzes with student scores
- Case Study and Exercises
- Options for hands-free or manual course navigation

Sentryx
1812 Samuelson Circle
Mississauga, ON
L5N 7Z5 Canada
Email: info@sentryx.com
Phone: 1 800 869 8460
Web: www.sentryx.com

For more information visit www.sentryx.com